liveeatcook**healthy**

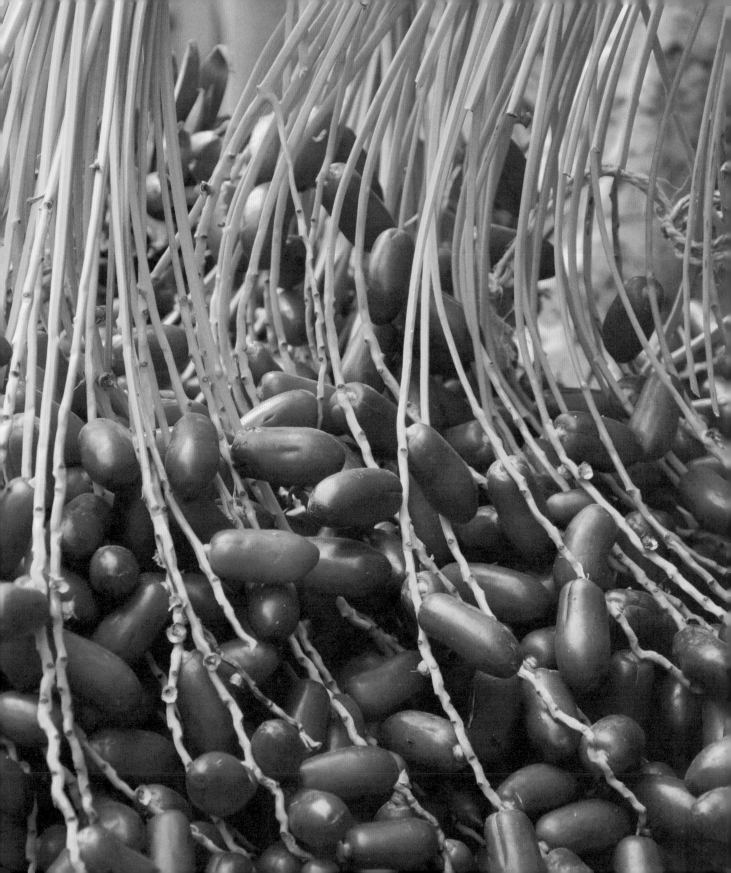

**Simple, Fresh, and Delicious Recipes
for Balanced Living**

liveeatcook**healthy**

RACHEL KHANNA

RECIPE PHOTOGRAPHS by MERVIN CHUA

Other Photographs by Rachel Khanna

DEDICATION

This book is dedicated to my husband, Jaideep, and daughters—Kieran, Anjali, Sophie, and Aaliya— without whom I never would have learned all that I did.

ACKNOWLEDGEMENTS

As with any work, there are always many hands that take part in the process. This is probably one of the few times when "many chefs" is a good thing! So, there are a number of people who I would like to thank for their help.

First of all, I would like to thank my mother, who taught me to never compromise when it comes to food and always encouraged and believed in me. I would also like to thank my husband, who kept asking me to recommend the one book that had all the information on eating and staying healthy, prompted me to sit down and create that book, and has always been my biggest fan. And my friend, Jean-Jacques, has always been a great source of advice and support.

I would also like to thank my friends, who encouraged me throughout the process and gave me invaluable feedback on the book. And a big thank you to all my family and friends who, sometimes willingly and sometimes unwillingly (but very graciously), tested my recipes. Another thank you to Annalyn Apostol, who helped me test all the recipes one last time.

I have had the honor of studying with Dr. Annemarie Colbin and Ina Niemann, and I admire them tremendously. They introduced me to a wealth of information about eastern and western medicine and healing practices. They also opened my eyes to the state of the food we eat and how important it is to stay balanced.

Finally, I would also like to thank Erica Sanders-Foege and Elizabeth Behrens for their tireless work on this book, and for making sure that not one tablespoon was omitted! I want to give an extra special thank you to Teresa Fernandes, who spent countless hours designing the book and making sure that each page was perfect. Teresa's eye for beauty and detail is unsurpassed!

—Rachel Khanna

Art Director: Teresa Fernandes,
  TFD STUDIO

Editor: Erica Sanders-Foege,
  WOODSIDE CREATIVE, LLC

Copy Editor: Elizabeth Behrens

Recipe Photographer: Mervin Chua,
  APERTURE

Prop Stylist: Jazreel Chan

Other Photographs: Rachel Khanna

MY JOURNEY TO WELLNESS BEGAN in my mid-30s when I was running a catering business. After I had children, four of them, I decided to go to culinary school to become a professional chef. I did, learned a lot, and had a great time. Eventually, I opened an organic food delivery service. The funny thing is that while I was cooking healthy foods for my clients, I was "nourishing" my body on energy bars that were full of sugar and very little of anything else because I was so busy trying to run the business. It was then that I realized that something was off. I wasn't terribly sick, but I was experiencing a latent feeling of unease; I was not at my best. I started getting colds, felt severely fatigued, and had frequent mood swings, migraine headaches, and night sweats. I chalked it up to the stress of work and kids, and figured it would go away soon. I had always been a strong person and refused to accept that anything could seriously affect me.

One snowy day, while driving home from the kitchen, I had a car accident. I was fatigued and not focused on the road. In retrospect, I realize that the car accident was a sign from the universe telling me to slow down and bring more balance into my life. It was through the power of food, specifically through eating the foods that properly nourished my body that I eventually regained my health.

I closed my business and decided to take a step back, to focus on educating others about healthy eating and in the process educated myself too. I went back to school and became a certified health counselor through the Institute of Integrative Nutrition™. I also completed training in food therapy from the Natural Gourmet Institute. The more I learned, the more I wanted to learn and I then enrolled in a program to earn a Ph.D. in Holistic Health. Interestingly, I discovered that there was a whole field of information out there that many doctors never seemed to talk about. Using food to heal instead of pills? What a novel concept!

I also learned about herbs and eastern healing methods. As I researched my symptoms, I came up with everything from chronic fatigue syndrome to fibro-myalgia to menopause—at 37! After months of going from one doctor to another, my food therapy teacher, Dr. Annemarie Colbin, said to me, "Your adrenals are depleted. You are tired from having had four children and you need to strengthen your kidneys. Eat more meat and take a vacation." Sure enough, I had been under stress (as we all are at times) and my system was in constant fight-or-flight mode. When this happens, the first thing to stop functioning properly is the digestive system, which means that your body stops absorbing important nutrients and your immune system starts to weaken. In the end, you become susceptible to all sorts of ailments.

So, I took a short break, added more meat and vegetables to my diet, and minimized my sugar intake. Slowly, my symptoms started going away. What Dr. Colbin proved to me, above all else, was that food—not pills—can be used to heal the body. In my case, once I really started to listen to my body, I gained insight as to what was happening and what my body needed. Intelligent things these bodies we have! Our bodies are sophisticated mechanisms that are composed of systems, each in balance with the others. If we push them too hard without giving back they shut down. So it was that just by eating whole foods—nothing processed, nothing refined, and no supplements—I began to feel a lot better. At the same time, my husband stopped getting seasonal allergies. And when I removed the sugar and the processed foods from all of our diets, my kids were less moody and distracted and didn't get as many colds. It seemed strange that such simple changes in the way our family ate and approached food could have such a large impact, but they did.

I hope that my hard-won experience speaks to you, too. Perhaps you are reading this because you can relate. Even if you try just a few of the things I recommend, you will be doing you and your family a great service. Or if you are interested in simply cooking more healthfully, there are loads of wonderfully healing recipes in Part Three.

It is so difficult to keep life in balance. I'm honored that you have decided to take the time to explore the method that works for me.

Be well,
Rachel

CONTENTS

thinkhealthy

Make a Plan

Identify those foods that are healthful to you,
and bring real foods back into your life.
When you do, your body will find its balance,
and you will reclaim your health,
vitality, and well-being.

THROUGH STUDIES AND PERSONAL EXPERIENCE, I've learned that so many of our illnesses are due to the food we eat. My belief is that the poor quality of much of the food that is marketed and sold to us in grocery stores is one of the leading causes of contemporary health issues, in particular diabetes, cancer, and developmental disorders. Processed and refined foods, foods laden with pesticides, hormones, and antibiotics, and genetically modified foods* are making us sick. At the same time, we are taking less time to be conscious of what we are putting into our bodies and how we nourish ourselves. One result is that we are gaining weight.

According to the Centers for Disease Control and Prevention (CDC), during the past 20 years, there has been a dramatic increase in obesity in the United States and rates remain high. In 2011, no state had a prevalence of obesity less than 20%.[1] This increase in obesity is occurring not only in the United States but also throughout the world. Interestingly, in developing countries (such as India and China), it is the upper classes that are becoming obese, because they increasingly have access to processed foods, many coming from western countries. Obesity often leads to diabetes, heart disease, hypertension, and many more illnesses.

---

* Genetically modified foods are those which have been created using genes from different types of foods or even species, such as creating a frost-resistant tomato by inserting fish genes into the vegetable's genetic makeup. See Part Two for more information on this topic.

Similarly, food sensitivities and asthma are also on the rise, especially in children.[2] Even if these are not directly related to our diets, the food we eat weakens our immune systems, and we are rendered more susceptible to these types of diseases. Many of the cures for these diseases and others we see today can be found in food. It is imperative to find ways to eat that are suitable to us individually. The purpose of this book is to show you how easy it is to identify those foods that are healthful to you, and bring real foods back into your life. When you do, your body will find its balance, and you will reclaim your health, vitality, and well-being.

3 Steps to Solid Nutrition

THE PROCESS TO FINDING BALANCE is not a difficult one. It just takes some commitment and dedication. But it doesn't happen overnight. Lasting change takes time, so be patient. A teacher once told me that the small changes you make on a daily basis have the most impact on your life. So begin with baby steps. There are three parts to start this process of reclaiming your health, vitality, and well-being.

STEP 1: REASSESS

If you're like me, you may be trying to take care of the kids, run your life, and be a good partner to your spouse. This is a lot to juggle and I often have trouble finding time to take care of everything. Frequently, the last person I have time for is myself. It's important to ask yourself, "Is the balance missing in my life?" Fixing your situation will take effort, but the good news is, the first step is do nothing.

That's right, take a moment and just breathe. Let your mind become as blank as you can make it. Get off the wheel, stop what you're doing, then slowly take time to figure out where you are and how you feel. What do you need to nourish yourself physically, emotionally, and mentally so you can stay healthy and strong? Set aside a few hours to simply take stock. You may even want to discuss this with your family to see how they are feeling, though it is always best to start with yourself. As the prime caretaker of the family, you need to focus on yourself before you can take care of anyone else.

Go somewhere where you will not be interrupted and focus on how you are feeling at that specific moment: Are you often fatigued? How are you sleeping? Are you irritable or angry? Do you feel like a hamster in a wheel? Do you get sick more than you think you should?

Then, think about how you would like to feel: Do you want to feel energized in the morning? Do you want to have less on your plate (figuratively and literally)? Do you just want to have a good night's sleep?

Now comes a challenge: Try to recall, then write down, the foods you eat on a regular basis. Think about the food that may be making you feel this way. Are you eating a lot of sugar? Refined and/or processed foods? Too much or not enough food? Too much or not enough of a specific food, such as meat or fruit? Once you've answered these questions, you have a base from which to start.

Sometimes when I do this exercise, I am overwhelmed with feelings of regret about how much more I should be doing or things I haven't made time for. It takes strength to push these thoughts from my mind. You may find this happening to you. As I said before, long-lasting change takes time, so don't let negative thoughts get you off track.

Many people don't have a clue as to how to start thinking about this. It took me years to reach the point where I feel I have a clear picture of how food affects me. You may be among those who do not know how to think about their eating and how it affects their energy, enjoyment of daily life, and overall health. When you are reassessing your lifestyle and the food that fuels it, consider these things:

Your Personal History. First, it is important to develop a general mindfulness about your body. In particular, think about your ancestry. What is your cultural background? Also, it's especially important to consider how you feel when you eat certain foods. For instance, do you feel energized when you eat sugar but then fatigued? Our bodies are not simple organisms. They have evolved to do many complex tasks, from breathing to growing to fighting bacteria. We do not know precisely how specific foods interact with our bodies. This is why one person's food can be another person's junk food. Your ancestry will help to determine why some foods may be more difficult to digest, and why some foods might be particularly beneficial because every culture has specific dietary traditions that have evolved around a specific environment and are adapted to that environment. In a sense, they are in your genes!

Again, take me for example. I am of German origin, where dairy is a part of the diet and has been for thousands of years. It's safe to assume that the German body has evolved in its environment to the climate and type of foods available to make this so. I am able to not only digest dairy but actually occasionally *need* dairy products such as cheese, especially to counter the effects of eating inflammatory foods — that is, foods which fuel inflammation in the body — such as eggplant, tomatoes, peppers, potatoes, also known as nightshade vegetables.

Similarly, because I am not originally from a warm climate, it takes my body time to adjust to different environments. In a funny example, my family and I moved to tropical Singapore from Connecticut in autumn, where, at the time we moved, the weather was turning cold and the days were growing shorter. In our new home I started cooking the warming foods that we normally eat in the fall. However, I noticed that I constantly felt hot and irritable. I was experiencing increased sensitivity to little things and not able to pinpoint a specific ailment. I decided to see a doctor certified in traditional Chinese medicine (TCM) and acupuncture who said that I had too much heat in my body. Indeed, the chili, sauerkraut, and beef stew were too warming for my body! I suppose if I had still been in Connecticut I would have felt fine.

So, food has a different effect on everyone. If you know your cultural heritage, consider how it might play a role in how your body reacts to food. And remember that whether or not you have information about your background, it is essential to pay attention to how you feel when you eat certain foods.

Making some of these changes might seem overwhelming at first, and you may feel that there is nothing left that you can eat. Don't get discouraged: Take your time. Try to eliminate one food that might be harming you and including one whole food—such as a new vegetable that you have never tried, more fruit, a different kind of grain or bean—one week at a time. Alternatively, try to replace some of the foods that might be detrimental to your health with healthier versions—for instance, you can reduce your intake of sugar by substituting sweetners like brown rice syrup or maple syrup, or you can substitute milk with almond milk in your morning coffee. Make sure to track your changes so you can assess how you feel after a week or a month.

STEP 2: TAKE CONTROL

Once you have assessed how you're feeling and have a list of suspected trigger foods, it's time to make changes in your lifestyle and eating habits. You control your health and, to some degree, your family's health. What are the foods that you need to incorporate into your life to make you feel better? What are the foods that you need to remove? This is a very individual process, and the best way to figure it out is by trial and error.

There are some foods that are more likely to trigger ill effects than others:

- Factory-farmed meat, poultry, and farmed fish, which are high in hormones and antibiotics
- Gluten (found in wheat, rye, barley, and sometimes, oats)
- Non-organic dairy products
- Refined and processed foods
- Sugar and artificial sweeteners
- Transfats

Have you noticed that when you eat sugar, you feel fatigued the following day? Try eliminating sugar from your diet for a week and see how you feel. Once you do, you feel so much better and eventually find that you no longer crave it.

Or perhaps you feel bloated when you eat bread. Consider eliminating it and all gluten from your diet for a week and see how you feel. Is your digestion better? Do you have more energy?

Alternatively, consider limiting your intake of dairy products for a few days and see how you feel. Does your runny nose and the tickle in the back of your throat go away?

STEP 3: MAKE AN EATING PLAN

Consider the rest of this book your main source for making an eating plan. In the meantime, here's *how* you make that plan.

Sometimes making a plan means getting rid of things you really like. You have to decide whether you are ready to make that commitment. It also means taking time to shop and plan meals. Time that you may not think you have. It will indeed take time at the beginning, but once you get into a habit and learn to stock a healthy pantry and refrigerator, it will be second nature. In the end, your life will be so much simpler.

So, here are a few tips:

1. First of all, determine what is keeping you from feeling great and get rid of it or, at the very least, decrease your intake. Avoid eating anything from your cupboards that is processed or loaded with sugar. And don't give it to anyone else – if it's not going to nourish you, it won't nourish anyone else either. Sugar is probably the hardest thing to give up because it is so addictive. The good news is that you can get rid of sugar without eliminating all things sweet. It is natural to like things that taste sweet, but it is not natural to eat sugar all the time. Replace the sugar with dried fruit, such as dates (my personal favorite), or a baked good made with less-refined sugars, such as Everyone's Favorite Maple Bars (*see recipe on pp. 87-88*).

2. Go to the supermarket and start reading the labels. Okay, the first time you do this, it will take you *hours*! But after a few times you will be whizzing through. A good rule of thumb is to stay on the perimeter of the store. That's where all the whole, real foods are. Sometimes you do need to go to a few different stores to get what you need, but if you can stock your pantry with the basics, you can limit your trips to the grocery store to a few times a week.

3. Whole foods are more costly in the short term, but I always like to think about all the money I am saving on doctor's bills and medication.

4. Take time to plan your meals. I usually sit down on Sunday night and plan my meals for the week. That way, I am not running to the grocery store at the last minute trying to find things for dinner. I generally plan two vegetarian days, a day or two for fish, a day for lamb or beef, and a day or two for chicken. On days when I am busy, I will plan for something quick, such as Thai Chicken in a Green Curry Sauce (*see recipe on p. 145*) and rice. On the other hand, on

days when I have more time, I will plan to make something more elaborate, such as Grilled Lamb Loin with Salsa Verde (*see recipe on p. 154*) and vegetables.

5. Meals don't have to be complex to be nourishing. Also, you don't have to eat foods that are foreign to you. When I had my catering business, people would ask me about the food I cooked and when I replied that it was all organic, they would grimace. You can make organic spaghetti Bolognese! Just because you incorporate healthy foods into your diet, it does not mean you will be eating "weird" foods.

6. Finally, take it easy on yourself. Do the best you can as often as you can and give yourself a break if you aren't perfect all the time, because nobody is. This is an important part of the process. We are all human. Use your mistakes as learning opportunities. As I mentioned before, lasting change takes time. So, if you really feel like treating yourself to that special dessert, do it.

Alternative Approaches to Finding Balance

EASTERN CULTURES HAVE A GREAT WAY OF LOOKING AT THIS through ancient healing methods: the Indians have ayurveda, which is a healing system based on lifestyle, yoga, meditation, and healthy eating. The Chinese have traditional Chinese medicine (TCM), which incorporates acupuncture, acupressure, *qi qong*, and healing herbs. Both are based on achieving a state of balance between the body and the universe.

Ayurveda is an ancient and complex medical methodology native to India that, in general terms, says within each body a unique balance exists and *prana*, or life force, flows. When there is imbalance, the flow of *prana* is interrupted and we become ill.

Ayurveda is based on the five elements: ether, air, water, fire, and earth. Within this scheme, there are three *doshas*, which are made up of combinations of these elements. *Vata* is the combination of ether and air; *pitta* is the combination of fire and water; and *kapha* is the combination of water and earth. Everything on earth, including human beings, is one of these *doshas*, or a combination of *doshas*. Therefore, each human being has his or her own state of balance. Occasionally, there might be an imbalance due to excess of a particular *dosha*. The key then is to bring one's *dosha* back into balance and to restore the flow of *prana* in our bodies.

For instance, I am primarily a *pitta dosha*, which is fire and water. *Pittas* are hot, sharp, oily, and light. They are also organized and goal-oriented, but they tend to take on a lot (imagine a fire burning a whole house). One of my teachers once said,

HEALTHY LIVING TIPS

In addition to food, there are a few other things I have changed in my life that have improved my health. In many traditional healing systems, such as homeopathy, ayurveda, and traditional Chinese medicine (TCM), what is fundamental to health is maintaining balance. This requires you to focus on your body and to notice when it is out of balance. The hardest thing about this is that it takes time and many of us aren't willing to stop and check in until we're already sick. So, just as you regularly maintain your house by checking the pipes, fixing leaks in the roof, or giving your home a new coat of paint, you should check your body and see how you feel.

When it comes to our diets, we often hear about some great new superfood and think this is carte blanche to ingest unlimited amounts. One minute it was cabbage, then it was goji and açai berries, then it was cocoa milk. Or we think that a new diet is going to improve our health. Several years back it was the Atkins diet and we all shunned bread, thinking that it would improve our lives. Then, the South Beach diet came around and told us the opposite.

Remember: everything in moderation. Let me stress, this is not meant to be a complex process. Just take a moment before preparing or eating a meal to determine how you think these foods will affect you and another moment after eating these foods to assess how you feel. It's always about finding balance in the body. Too much of any one thing will cause an imbalance.

"*Pittas* get hit hard and get knocked to their knees." Well, in my case, she wasn't kidding. It was after I had knee surgery and several months after my car accident, when I had time to think about all that I was feeling emotionally and physically. I realized that I needed to slow down. I realized that my *pitta* was out of balance and I needed to do more things to bring it back into balance. Because *pittas* represent fire, they need things to cool the fire. So they need to avoid excess heat and to eat cooling and raw foods. They should also pursue activities that are cooling, such as swimming. Similarly, the word *vata* originates from the word "to move" and that is what identifies a *vata* body type – constant motion. *Vata* people are creative and joyful but when out of balance can be unfocused, ungrounded, or anxious (imagine the wind blowing). People who are predominantly a *vata* body type need to keep warm and calm, avoid raw and other cooling foods, and eat warming foods and spices.

Finally, *kapha dosha* types are grounded and stable, just like the earth. When in excess, *kapha* people can get lazy and sluggish, or emotionally needy. Think of something getting stuck in the mud and becoming immobile. *Kaphas* need to exercise and keep moving. They should avoid heavy or oily foods, or foods that can create blockages (such as dairy), and eat more foods that are light and drying.[3]

Dr. Vasant Lad, a well-known ayurvedic practitioner, has developed a detailed list of foods that are suited to each *dosha*. If this traditional healing modality is of interest to you, I highly recommend that you read his books. As a general guide, *vatas* do well with sweet fruit, cooked vegetables, dairy products, fish, and meat. They should avoid dried fruit, raw or dried vegetables, wheat and oat products, most beans, and game meat. *Pittas* do well with sweet fruit, sweet and bitter vegetables, most grains and beans, and dairy products. They should stay away from sour fruit, pungent vegetables, fish, and nuts. Finally, *kaphas* should eat astringent foods, pungent and bitter vegetables, most grains and beans, and primarily white meats. They should avoid sweet and sour fruit and vegetables, yeasted breads and rice, red meats and seafood, and nuts.

The main thing to understand is everyone's body is different — I am a *pitta dosha*, and my daughters are predominantly *vata* and *kapha*. We need different things to stay in balance. This idea of everyone having his or her own state of homeostasis is crucial and reinforces the idea that we need to do everything in moderation to maintain our state of equilibrium. Ayurveda is not the only medical model that looks at balance as essential to good health.

In TCM, the universe is broken down into five elements: wood, fire, earth, metal, and water. These elements interact with and influence one another. In the human body, these elements exist in combinations, with one usually dominant. At times, one element may be deficient or in excess, causing imbalance. Because foods are part of the universe, they, too, are broken down into the elements of wood, fire, earth, metal, and water. If you look on the chart "TCM and The Five Characteristic Elements," on pp. 24-25, you can see which foods fall under the different categories. Assess your diet, and if you are sensing an imbalance, try to determine which foods may be the cause. There may also be other causes, such as the environment you are in or emotional issues, but food is always a good place to start. When you eat a balanced diet incorporating foods from the five elements, then it is quite likely that your body will find a state of equilibrium.

Entrepreneur Steve Jobs, who passed away from pancreatic cancer in 2011, is a perfect example of someone whose body was most likely out of balance, according to the teachings of the Four Pillars of Destiny, the Chinese philosophy. He was born on February 24, 1955, at 7:15 p.m. The configuration of his elements, based on Chinese theory, makes him almost all "earth." As we can see from the chart on pp. 24-25, the earth element is manifest as imagination and creativity, and, regarding the parts of the body, earth is associated with the liver, spleen, and

The 5 Elements in Traditional Chinese Medicine

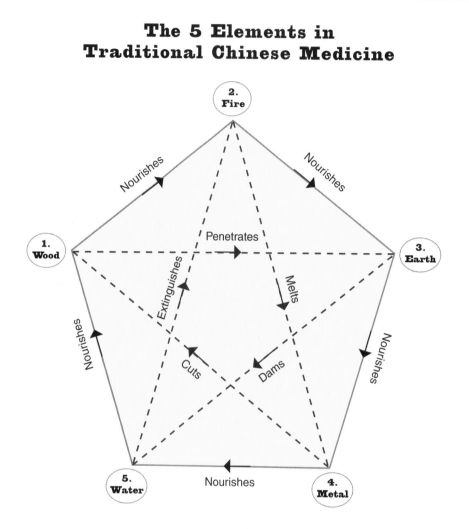

pancreas. So when many of the elements are determined to be "earth," as Jobs's were, one may have the potential to be very creative and have issues with one's liver, spleen, and/or pancreas.

Moreover, it seems that Jobs ate foods primarily from the earth category. According to his official biography, *Steve Jobs* by Walter Isaacson, apparently, he went through periods when he ate only fruit, sometimes just carrots and apples.[4] Naturally, this would have worsened his already unbalanced elements. Of course, this is an extreme example, and most people's configuration of elements is not this skewed towards one element, but it demonstrates how an imbalance in elements can affect someone physically.

The simplest method to find out your configuration of elements is the following, using the chart on pp. 24-25:

Step 1: Assess your preferences (colors, seasons, foods).

Step 2: Determine which parts of your body tend to be affected when you might be out of balance. Do you tend to have problems with digestion, elimination, or your bones?

Step 3: Determine which emotions resonate with you. Are you more likely to get angry, fearful or anxious?

The results could signify that one of the elements is in excess or, conversely, is deficient. With the help of the diagram on p. 22, guide your eating to the elements that will bring your body back into balance. If you're eating too much or too little of one element, find the element that balances by looking at the one that mitigates it (if too much) or "feeds" it (if too little). There are also many great books that help you assess your configuration. Two that I recommend are: *Chinese Medicine for Maximum Immunity* by Jason Elias and Katherine Ketchum and *Power of the Five Elements* by Charles Moss. In my case, I have a lot of metal and earth. When I am out of balance, I tend to get angry. This is because the excess metal mitigates my wood element and the wood element manifests itself with anger and shouting. Similarly, I tend to crave green foods which fall into the wood category. This is my body's way of telling me that I am lacking the wood element and need to replenish it by eating wood foods.

Again, the gist of these traditional healing methods is that our bodies have a state of balance that they revert to. When we are out of balance, our bodies give us signals, and it is imperative that we take note of them and bring our bodies back into balance. If we don't, we risk getting more severe, chronic symptoms. While the whole process of choosing foods to suit one's dosha or elements seems a little complex, it really is not. If you are preparing balanced meals with a mixture of vegetables, grains, and meats or fish, then there is a way for everyone in the family to find balance. You will also find that children are particularly adept at intuitively choosing the foods they need.

When preparing foods, I try to incorporate different flavors and colors to make sure that everyone's plate is balanced and that there is something on the table to suit everyone's needs. Ayurveda and TCM have different recommendations for the body, so I find it best to refer to just one system. If one of these systems speaks to you, I suggest that you read up on it. However, if you are incorporating whole foods into your diet and eating a wide variety of fruits, vegetables, grains, beans, meats, and seafood, then you will most likely already be in balance.

TCM and the Five Characteristic Elements

Type >	1. Wood	2. Fire
CHARACTERISTICS	SENSORY: green, sour ENVIRONMENTAL: spring EMOTIONAL: anger, impatience, shouting CORPOREAL: liver, gall bladder MANIFESTATION: purification, cleansing, planning, decision making	SENSORY: red, bitter, touch ENVIRONMENTAL: summer EMOTIONAL: joy, laughter, anxiety, excessive talking CORPOREAL: circulation, heart, small intestine, vascular system MANIFESTATION: commanding to action, speech
ASSOCIATED PARTS OF THE BODY	eyes: sight shoulders muscles: action nails	complexion pituitary gland tongue
LEGUMES	green lentils split peas limas	red lentils
VEGETABLES	bland green vegetables sprouts broccoli string beans carrots zucchini lettuces	asparagus red bell pepper bitter greens tomatoes Brussels sprouts endive
FRUITS	avocados citrus tart apples	apricots raspberries strawberries
ANIMAL PRODUCTS	butter liver chicken sour yogurt cream	lamb shrimp
MISCELLANEOUS	barley olives vinegar cashews rye wheat fats sauerkraut wheat germ oats sour pickles	amaranth ketchup sesame beer liquor sunflower chocolate pistachios tobacco coffee popcorn wine corn quinoa

Based on 5 *Phases of Food*, Copyright 2009, Pathways4Health, derived from J.W. Garvy, Jr. @1983 and Annemarie Colbin, Ph.D.

Assess your preferences and which parts of your body are affected when you're out of balance. Then, with the help of the diagram on p. 22, select foods according to the elements below that will bring your body into balance.

3. Earth

SENSORY: yellow, orange, sweet, taste
ENVIRONMENTAL: Indian summer
EMOTIONAL: sympathy, worry
CORPOREAL: Thymus: mouth, digestion, stomach, spleen, pancreas, lips
MANIFESTATION: imagination

4. Metal

SENSORY: white, hot, pungent
ENVIRONMENTAL: autumn
EMOTIONAL: grief, weeping, sadness
CORPOREAL: respiration, lungs, large intestine
MANIFESTATION: establishing order

5. Water

SENSORY: deep blue, brown, black, salty
ENVIRONMENTAL: winter
EMOTIONAL: courage, vitality, will power, fear, groaning
CORPOREAL: kidneys and bladder
MANIFESTATION: elimination, learning

Earth		Metal		Water	
flesh		thyroid	body	adrenals	teeth
muscle tone		nose	hair	ears	head: hair
lips		skin		bones and marrow	knees and ankles
chickpeas		all white beans	tempeh	aduki beans	
		soybeans		black beans	
		tofu		kidney beans	
chard	spaghetti squash	all sharp white roots	celery	onion	beets	mushrooms
collards	spinach	cabbage	chile peppers	radishes	burdock	all seaweeds
parsnips	sweet orange vegetables	cauliflower	garlic	rape	kale	
pumpkin	sweet corn		ginger	turnips		
rutabagas	winter squashes					
sweet apples	grapes	peaches		blackberries	cranberries
bananas	mangos	pears		blueberries	watermelon
cantaloupe	papayas			concord grapes	
coconut	pineapples				
dates	prunes				
figs					
anchovies	salmon	beef	all white fish	bluefish	kidney
cottage cheese	swordsfish	cheese	turkey	caviar	pork
ice cream	tuna	egg whites		duck	sardines
milk				ham	all shell fish
almonds	pecans	bay leaf	tofu	buckwheat	salt
barley malt	pumpkin seeds	black pepper	spirulina	chestnuts	tamari
honey	sugar: white and brown	cayenne	walnuts	kasha	tekka
maple syrup	sweet potatoes	rice	white potatoes	miso	
millet		tempeh			

Getting Rid of Wastes and Building Up Immunity

PEOPLE UNDERESTIMATE HOW IMPORTANT the elimination of wastes such as heavy metals and chemicals, environmental toxins, and bacteria, is to our health. If we are unable to eliminate the toxins we accumulate on a daily basis, we create blockages that, over time, will cause disease. Research shows that most illnesses are the result of excess toxins in the body. So when I speak of imbalance, I'm not talking only about stress and fatigue but also about accumulated toxins in the body. Simply put, there is not enough good stuff to balance the bad, so you get sick. This is why it is so important to make sure that your digestive system is functioning well. This is also why the minute you start including refined and processed foods in your diet you then start to create blockages in the flow of energy, deplete your body of essential nutrients, and cause imbalance.

I realized that much of the reason I was getting sick was because the stress I had been under had depleted my adrenals, which, in turn, did not allow me to absorb the nutrients I was consuming. Moreover, when I was consuming poor-quality nutrients, such as those in energy bars, my body wasn't being nourished as it needed to be.

Good digestion and regular detoxification, by drinking plenty of water and incorporating cleansing foods such as arugula, dandelion greens, parsley, and cilantro are important to help keep the liver and kidneys functioning properly. Your liver makes bile, which is essential to the digestion of fats. Moreover, the liver removes toxic chemicals from the bloodstream. In addition, the kidneys are in charge of eliminating cellular wastes from the body through the urine. Because these two organs are crucial in eliminating wastes, it is important to keep them functioning well.

HOME REMEDIES

There are days when you will be under the weather or a bug will have gotten the better of you. At times like these, it is really important to eat healthfully and get plenty of rest to nourish your body and strengthen your immune system. Here are some common ailments and the simple home remedies I like to use:

- **Cold**
  Chicken soup
  (see recipe on p. 117)

- **Diarrhea**
  Mash a banana and mix with
  one grated apple.

- **Earache**
  Put a hot compress on
  the affected ear.

- **Sore throat**
  Combine the juice of one lemon
  with hot water and 1 Tbsp. honey.

I cleanse on a daily basis by giving my body enough time to eliminate waste. I do this by eating dinner early and giving my body at least 12 hours before I have breakfast the next day. We also eat vegetarian foods at least once a week. I will occasionally do a juice cleanse by drinking just juices for three days, but only when I feel I have indulged; you don't want to use a cleanse as an excuse to "pig out." Other cleansing options are to eat only fruit or vegetables for several days. The idea is to give your liver and kidneys a break by eating simple foods. No matter what program you undertake, please consult a physician before embarking on any detoxification.

AIDING GOOD DIGESTION

Abstaining from unhealthy foods isn't the only way to keep your body in balance. You can aid good digestion by eating foods that actively help the body eliminate toxins. Some of these foods are:

- Bitter greens such as arugula, dandelion greens, green cabbage, broccoli, and Brussels sprouts

- Parsley, cilantro, and Brazil nuts

- Peas, leafy greens, and root vegetables that are bitter and astringent

The Role of Inflammation

ONE OF THE MOST IMPORTANT KEYS to good health is minimizing inflammation. There is so much to be said on the topic that it has filled whole books. Here, I'll try just to sketch the basic issues. Inflammation is the body's response to injury. It can cause an imbalance in the body when it goes out of control. In other words, the body has a tendency to overreact when it senses an injury that needs to be repaired. Inflammation can be caused by actual injuries inside or outside the body like bruising or infection, but it can also be caused by and worsened when eating poor-quality foods. A poor diet can create an inflammatory condition when none existed or worsen a pre-existing inflammatory condition. Similarly, an imbalanced system causes increased stress on organs and tissues and can contribute to further inflammation and/or injury. It can be a vicious cycle when an imbalanced system causes an inflammatory reaction that, in turn, causes further imbalances.

Swelling, redness, bruising are all inflammatory reactions. They indicate that there is increased blood flow to the injured area containing white blood cells, hormones, and neurotransmitters. Therefore, some inflammation is important because it is the body's signal that it is trying to repair itself.

Chronic inflammation is ongoing and less intense. It can be set in motion when you are exposed to environmental toxins, chemicals, viruses, bacteria, food allergens, and stress. These trigger the body's inflammatory response because the body senses it is being attacked. In particular, when you are under a lot of mental or emotional stress, your body, sensing the need to be ready for fight or flight, releases stress hormones such as adrenaline. If this is a constant state, your system eventually shuts down nonessential processes in order to deal with a perceived threat, specifically the digestive and reproductive processes. Hence, the body produces chemicals that cause redness and swelling on a cellular level. This is when we get inflammatory conditions such as asthma, arthritis, psoriasis, fibromyalgia, chronic fatigue syndrome, heart disease, and many more conditions.

It is often difficult to tell what causes an inflammatory response because we are faced with so many potential triggers at any given time. This is why it is important to nourish ourselves properly. We need to be able to mitigate any inflammatory response in our bodies when it occurs. The best way to do this is by eating healthy foods.

INFLAMMATORY FOODS

It is important to avoid inflammatory foods. Some of these triggers I have mentioned above:

- Alcohol, caffeine, soda

- Artificial sweeteners

- Factory-farmed meats and poultry

- Nightshade vegetables (potatoes, tomatoes, peppers, eggplant)*

- Refined and processed foods

- Sugar (white sugar, high-fructose corn syrup, all of it...)

- Transfats and other inflammatory oils such as corn oil, safflower/sunflower oil, cottonseed oils

* While some nightshade vegetables are good because they are high in antioxidants, they are also high in alkaloids that might trigger inflammation. For instance, if I eat too many nightshade vegetables, I notice that my knees feel sore. So a food that may be good for one person may not be the best for another.

ANTI-INFLAMMATORY FOODS

Below are some foods that help keep inflammation in balance:

- Avocados

- Foods rich in Omega-3 fatty acids (fish, especially anchovies and sardines, walnuts, flax seeds)

- Ginger, turmeric

- Grass-fed meat, free-range poultry

- Leafy green vegetables

- Olive oil, coconut oil

- Pineapples, which are high in bromelain (an enzyme which minimizes inflammation)

- Seaweeds

- Whole grains

The Role of Antioxidants

THE FINAL ELEMENT TO GOOD HEALTH is consuming plenty of antioxidants. Consider that everything in the universe is made up of matter, which is made up of atoms. Atoms, in turn, contain protons and electrons. Free radicals are atoms or molecules with unpaired electrons. Electrons prefer to be in pairs in order to be more stable and will, therefore, when unpaired, try to take electrons from other atoms or molecules to create a pair. This sets off a chain reaction of unpaired electrons trying to pair with other electrons. The unpaired electrons are called free radicals and can cause severe damage to our cells because they are trying to "grab" electrons from other cells, thus creating an imbalance. Free radicals fuel inflammation because they impair cell functions by interrupting the transport of substances in and out of cells, and by creating excesses and deficiencies of proteins the body needs. Free radicals come from environmental, chemical, and other pollutants, and occasionally, from our own bodies. They cause oxidation of our cells, which is damaging to them.

Think of a group of cells in the body as a peeled apple. If the apple is left out on the counter, over the course of a few hours it will turn brown. The same thing will happen to the group of cells when it encounters free radicals from toxins or pollutants in the environment, or from chemicals in our food.

In most cases, the body can handle free radicals, but if it is weakened, if we do not have enough antioxidants, or if the free radicals are excessive, then there is damage to the cells and their functions. Antioxidants help prevent free radicals from damaging cells and causing inflammation. In essence, antioxidants move electrons around and pair electrons to free radicals, thus preventing the damaging chain reaction from taking place. This is why it is important to eat foods rich in antioxidants. So in the case of the brown apple, if you put lemon juice, which is rich in vitamin C, on the apple, it will not turn brown as quickly.

WHERE ANTIOXIDANTS ARE FOUND

There are many different kinds of healthy antioxidants. Here is a list of types of foods that contain them.

- Brightly colored fruits and vegetables
- Foods rich in vitamin C, such as citrus fruit, berries, bananas, kiwi, mango, cauliflower, broccoli, and asparagus
- Foods rich in vitamin E, such as nuts and seeds, tomatoes, kiwi, mango, and broccoli
- Foods rich in selenium, such as Brazil nuts, fish, liver, grass-fed beef, and mushrooms

Live, Eat, Cook Well

OKAY, SO WITH ALL THIS INFORMATION, how should we eat? Here are some rules of thumb that I follow:

WHOLE FOODS

Eat foods with whole ingredients. This means stay away from processed and refined foods. From a practical point of view, this means shop the perimeter of the supermarket where it's colder and where the fresh fruit and vegetables, meat, poultry, and fish tend to be located. The inner aisles of the supermarket are essentially for the processed foods. Eat foods that don't have long lists of ingredients.

During my certification in Food Therapy, I was taught to look at all foods as a whole. The carrot without the fiber is not a whole food; the egg without the yolk is not a whole food; the wheat without the bran and the germ is not a whole food. When you eat partial foods you don't get the full benefits of the entire organism. Not only that, organisms are so complex that we can't explain why things happen when certain variables are added or removed. So, when we refine foods (and strip things away or add things on), we are interfering with their natural order without necessarily knowing the consequences. Also, I believe our bodies do not recognize refined and processed food as sustenance.

VEGETABLES, VEGETABLES, AND MORE VEGETABLES

In general, we don't eat enough vegetables and fruit and would do well to incorporate more into our diets. There are two secondary rules to this one:

- Try to get as many foods as possible from local sources.

- If you get organic foods, you know that they haven't been grown using chemical fertilizers or pesticides, antibiotics, or hormones, and that they haven't been altered from their natural state.

GRASS-FED, FREE-RANGE, AND WILD

When you eat animals that are raised as nature intended, you get benefits beyond just the nutrient value of the food. It is my belief that when you purchase foods that have been factory-farmed, you not only get products loaded with hormones and antibiotics, you also get a lot of negative energy from how the animals were treated.

What to Avoid

THERE ARE FOODS THAT WILL NOT HELP YOU maintain balance, especially if your system is already stressed. In addition to processed foods, which I've already discussed, as much as possible, stay away from:

SUGARS

Processed foods contain added sugars as well as chemical preservatives so that they can remain on store shelves for extended periods of time. Those sugars and preservatives are detrimental to our health. Organic or not, sugar wreaks havoc on the immune and endocrine systems. As William Dufty notes in his book, *Sugar Blues*, "Refined sugar is lethal when ingested by humans because it provides only that which nutritionists describe as empty or naked calories. In addition, sugar is worse than nothing because it drains and leeches the body of precious vitamins and minerals through the demand its digestion, detoxification, and elimination make upon one's entire system."[5]

DAIRY

Dairy is a controversial product. First of all, a child doesn't need milk past the age of about five, when he/she should theoretically be weaned. After weaning, a child stops producing the enzymes necessary to digest milk. In addition, many of us have difficulty digesting dairy because when milk is processed and pasteurized, the enzyme that enables the digestion of milk –lactase– is removed. As Annemarie Colbin notes in her book *Food and Healing*, "The healing professions have finally noticed that many people have acute reactions to milk, including cramps, bloating, intestinal gas, and diarrhea."[6] Second, unless it's organic, most milk today is produced with genetically modified growth hormones and antibiotics, which are all absorbed by our systems. As previously discussed, it is also worthwhile to note that not many cultures can tolerate milk and dairy products. As Marion Nestle, author of *What to Eat*, notes, 75% of the world's adults are unable to digest lactose. Those who generally can are those of Northern European ancestry.[7]

MONOSODIUM GLUTAMATE AND OTHER FOOD ADDITIVES

Many chemicals are added to processed and refined foods, including artificial food coloring and flavor, artificial sweeteners, monosodium glutamate (MSG), nitrites, nitrates, sulfites, and other preservatives. These are generally added to prolong shelf life or otherwise enhance their salability. The problem is that they affect our health and, especially in the case of MSG, our brain function.

MSG is often used in Chinese and other Asian restaurants as a flavor enhancer instead of salt. Interestingly, Asians traditionally used kombu seaweed as a flavor enhancer.

I know immediately if I have eaten MSG because I get a headache and start feeling "off." Other typical reactions to MSG include tingling in the hands and feet and rapid heartbeat. MSG, which is made by fermenting tapioca starch, sugar cane, and sugar beets, is the monosodium salt of glutamic acid, an excitatory neurotransmitter. MSG, along with the artificial sweetener aspartate, is considered an excitotoxin, a substance that excites nerve cells literally to death. Russell L. Blaylock, M.D. notes in his book: *Excitotoxins: The Taste that Kills*, "Neuroscientists have discovered that glutamate is one of the most common neurotransmitters in the brain. Its role is primarily that of an excitatory substance, that is it causes the brain to be stimulated, much the way cocaine does."[8] Overstimulation of the brain leads to all sorts of neurological imbalances, such as tremors, seizures, learning, and emotional disorders.

MSG can be found in hydrolyzed protein, sodium caseinate, calcium caseinate, autolyzed yeast, yeast extract, and gelatin. Here is yet another reason to read the labels of the products you buy and, as much as possible, stay away from refined and processed foods.

WHITE FLOUR AND REFINED PRODUCTS

All products made with refined wheat or other refined grain products have the bran and germ removed. These parts of the plant are an important source of fiber. If we eat refined grain products without the fiber, the sugars get absorbed very quickly into our bodies, thereby creating imbalances in our blood sugar levels. Over time, our bodies weaken and become unable to manage the sudden spikes in blood sugar and the resulting insulin surges to metabolize it, leading to a whole host of diseases.

Nonfood Essentials

FINALLY, HERE ARE TWO OTHER THINGS that are paramount to good health:

EXERCISE

Get some exercise! Move your body. Exercise gets the blood flowing throughout the body so all the cells can be nourished. Exercise also helps bones and improves heart and lung health. Exercise removes toxins and regulates hormones.

SLEEP

We need to get six to eight hours of sleep a night. We tend to underestimate the importance of getting a good night's sleep. Sleep is crucial to our well-being because our bodies use the time to heal and revitalize, and lack of sleep can cause severe health problems, such as immune weakness, weight gain, lack of mental focus, and blood sugar imbalances.

Staying Healthy and Feeling Good

THIS IS A LOT OF INFORMATION, but in general, if you eat a diet rich in real foods that haven't been processed or refined, and that are as close to their natural state as possible, you will find that it is easy to stay healthy and feel good. Most important, incorporate loads of fruit and vegetables in your diet. In this way, it will be easier to maintain a state of balance.

You are in a position to take charge of your life and regain your health, energy, and vitality. You have assessed how you feel when you eat certain foods; you have assessed which foods are harmful to you and which are not; and you have committed to making some small but significant changes to your lifestyle and eating habits.

It's time to determine specifically what foods will nourish your body. In the next part, you will learn about where the food you eat comes from. Think of this as going on a tour of the grocery store/farmstand. Then, we will come home and cook!

TOP 25 HEALING FOODS

These are the top foods that I find the most healing. They are particularly beneficial against inflammation and oxidation, which I consider to be the two main causes of illness. But remember that all whole and natural foods have healing properties and are beneficial to your health.

1. Aduki beans
Of all the beans, aduki beans are my favorite because I find them easier to digest than most beans. They are a great source of fiber as well as B vitamins.

2. Avocados
In addition to potassium, avocados contain healthy monounsaturated and polyunsaturated fats and lots of fiber to help digestion.

3. Berries
Strawberries, blueberries, raspberries, blackberries, to name more than a few, are full of vitamin C, which is an important antioxidant.

4. Brazil Nuts
Brazil nuts are loaded with selenium, which, as I mentioned earlier, is an important antioxidant.

5. Broccoli and Cauliflower
These popular vegetables are members of the brassica family. Research has shown that vegetables in this family are very beneficial in preventing and fighting cancer.

6. Butternut Squash, Kabocha Squash, and Pumpkin
All members of the squash family, pumpkin, kabocha, and butternut squash are a great source of potassium, which helps maintain the electrolyte balance in the body.
    Squash is also a good source of fiber, which is essential for proper digestion and helps to regulate blood sugar levels.

7. Cilantro and Parsley
Cilantro and parsley, like other leafy greens, have a lot of chlorophyll, which helps eliminate toxins and heavy metals from the body. Cilantro and parsley are also good sources of vitamin D, which helps the body retain calcium.

8. Coconut
It is only when I moved to Southeast Asia that I discovered the full benefits of coconut. First of all, it is a very healthy fat. It also contains lauric acid, an antimicrobial, which explains why coconut is used in cooking in tropical climates. Finally, coconut contains a lot of potassium, a mineral that is crucial to maintaining the electrolyte balance in the body.

9. Eggs
Eggs are a great source of protein, and the yolks are full of Omega-3 fatty acids.

10. Garlic
It's no wonder garlic was used to ward off vampires. It is one of the healthiest foods to eat because it possesses antimicrobial and antibacterial properties, and is an antioxidant. Garlic also supports the immune system and helps detoxify the liver.

11. Ghee
Ghee is butter in which the milk solids have been boiled off. Also known as clarified butter, ghee is a healthy fat that helps the body absorb vitamins A, D, E, and K.
    It also contains selenium, an antioxidant mineral. In ayurveda, ghee is important for the healthy flow of fluids throughout the body and it is valued as a tonic for the mind, brain, and nervous system.

12. Ginger
Ginger is a great digestive aid and anti-inflammatory agent. Ginger also stimulates circulation.

13. Kale, Spinach, and Other Leafy Greens
Greens like kale and spinach are a great source of calcium and vitamins C, A, and K. Arugula and dandelion are cleansing greens that help remove toxins from the liver.

14. Kuzu
Kuzu is a Japanese root that helps support digestion. It is very calming and soothing.

15. Lemons
Lemons are a great source of vitamin C, which is an antioxidant and helps support the immune system. Vitamin C is also an effective liver tonic and helps the body detoxify.

16. Mushrooms
Mushrooms have been shown to help prevent and fight cancer, especially maitake and reishi mushrooms.

17. Onions, Leeks, Scallions, and Spring Onions
Like garlic, all types of onions possess antimicrobial and antioxidant properties. They also help fight inflammation.

18. Pineapple
Pineapple contains bromelain, an important anti-inflammatory nutrient.

19. Quinoa
The Incas have always considered quinoa a super-grain, meaning that its nutritional value is higher than that of other grains like oats and wheat. It is full of essential minerals and vitamins.

20. Sardines
You read it right. Sardines are one of my top healing foods! This is because they are full of Omega-3 fatty acids, which help in brain development, circulation, and heart health. They are also loaded with B vitamins and selenium.

21. Sauerkraut
It is essential to eat foods that support your digestive system because this is where your immune system fights most of its battles. Sauerkraut is a great source of beneficial bacteria (probiotics), a key player in the fight.
    Traditionally, fermented foods like kimchi (as well as sauerkraut) are excellent sources of probiotics. Sauerkraut is also high in anti-inflammatory properties.

22. Seaweed
Seaweed is a good source of iodine, which is key for the proper function of the thyroid. It also helps the body detoxify by reducing the uptake of radioactive particles.

23. Sweet Potatoes and Yams
Sweet potatoes and yams are another great source of fiber, and they also help fight inflammation. In Traditional Chinese Medicine, sweet potatoes are said to nourish the spleen, liver, blood, and qi.

24. Turmeric
Turmeric is a member of the ginger family and an anti-inflammatory spice.

25. Yogurt
Yogurt is another great probiotic that provides immune-supporting bacteria for the digestive system.

BRANDS I LIKE

I prefer to get fresh produce from local farms whenever I can. I like to support local farmers and get my ingredients when they are in their most nutritious state. The website www.localharvest.org has information on farmers' markets and sources for local food across the U.S. If I can't find local ingredients, then I buy organic ones from the local grocery store. Here is a list of the brands I like:

Arrowhead Mills is a company that produces organic grains and flours using traditional techniques. **www.arrowheadmills.com**

Bionaturae is an Italian company that has a nice line of organic foods used in Italian cuisine. **www.bionaturae.com**

Bob's Red Mill sells a wide variety of grains and flours, many of which are organic, produced using time-honored techniques, like grinding whole grains at cool temperatures with a stone mill. The company also sells beans. **www.bobsredmill.com**

Clearspring distributes European and Japanese food products that are created using traditional methods. **www.clearspring.co.uk**

Crown Prince is known for its high-quality canned seafood products. **www.crownprince.com**

Eden Foods sells a wide range of organic and all-natural European and Asian food products. **www.edenfoods.com**

Frontier Natural Products Co-op has a wonderful selection of organic spices, teas, and herbs. **www.frontiercoop.com**

Green & Black's is a good source for organic fair-trade chocolate. **www.greenandblacks.com**

Hain Pure Food Company produces a wide variety of all-natural and organic foods. **www.hainpurefoods.com**

Heritage Foods USA sells heritage-bred animals and poultry, such as turkeys and wild salmon. The company also has a line of high-quality food products. **www.heritagefoodsusa.com**

Lakewood Juices sells organic 100% juice products. **www.lakewoodjuices.com**

Lundberg Family Farms is a small family farm that grows rice in a sustainable manner. **www.lundberg.com**

Niman Ranch works with small family farmers and is a purveyor of, among other products, natural, sustainably, and humanely raised beef, lamb, pork, and poultry. **www.nimanranch.com**

Organic Valley is a farmer-owned cooperative that offers a range of primarily organic dairy foods. **www.organicvalley.coop**

Rustichella d'Abruzzo produces a wide variety of traditionally made pastas. **www.rustichella.it**

RW Knudsen Family sells organic juices that don't contain sugar, preservatives, or artificial colors. **www.rwknudsenfamily.com**

Spectrum sells high-quality organic and expeller-pressed oils and other products. **www.spectrumorganics.com**

Thai Kitchen is a great source for authentic Thai food products. **www.thaikitchen.com**

Tinkiyáda sells a wide variety of organic, brown rice pasta. **www.tinkyada.com**

choosehealthy

Get the Facts

*Even when we try to nourish ourselves with
what we consider to be healthy foods, they may not
actually be healthy. This is why it is so important—
now more than ever— to make the right choices
about foods to nourish our bodies.*

NOW THAT YOU'VE TAKEN THE TIME TO ASSESS YOUR LIFESTYLE and have come up with a plan for finding balance and eating healthy, it's time to learn more about your food options. In my research, I've come across good news and bad news. The good news is that there are many private and government groups that are interested in looking at the business of food—agriculture, farming, aquaculture, etc., so there's a lot of information available to us that wasn't before. The bad news is that the information isn't that, well, positive. Our food system itself, it seems, is out of balance.

The problem with our food system, as I see it, is that the business of growing food has become a commercial enterprise. As such, the ultimate goal of food manufacturers is to provide affordable food, regardless of the other costs attached, such as those related to health and the environment. Governments have long supported this goal. In the United States, for example, beginning in the 1930s, federal programs were enacted that ensured that grain producers received a fixed price if open market prices fell too low, and that sought to provide affordable lunches for school children. While on the one hand, these policies might initially have seemed honorable, the outcome is now detrimental to human health and the environment. And as a result, years later, this big business is responsible for polluting water systems and depleting the soils.

Our system produces food that is cheap to grow and costs less to the consumer but is, ultimately, inferior in quality. For example, this

substandard food is responsible, in part, for the increase of immune-resistant bacteria that thrive due to the high levels of chemicals used today in food production. Specifically, antibiotic use in cows to produce milk is thought to be one of the reasons we need stronger and stronger antibiotics to fend off disease. This is happening not just in the United States, but all over the world.

Because of the poor quality of food, even when we try to nourish our bodies with what we consider to be healthy foods, they may not actually be healthy. They may contain pesticides and fertilizers; they may contain genetically modified organisms; they may contain antibiotics; or they may be farmed in unsanitary conditions. This is why it is so important – now more than ever – to make the right choices about foods to nourish our bodies. Everything around us has energy, from plants to animals to humans, and when we raise or grow things with negative energy, we get negative energy in return. So, again, the key is to make the right choices about foods that will nourish our bodies.

Fruits and Vegetables

LET'S START WITH THE BUSINESS OF GROWING FRUITS AND VEGETABLES. I highly recommend eating organic fruits and vegetables because much of the commercially grown produce that we eat is treated with pesticides.

Farming is big business and has been for decades, meaning that fruits and vegetables are grown by a few large farms, which need massive amounts of potent chemicals to fight pests. According to a 2001 study by the U.S. Environmental Protection Agency, pesticides in general are a widespread problem. Each year, according to estimates from the study, 5.7 billion pounds of pesticides are released into the environment. [9] The pesticides in the study include all pesticides, not just those used in farming, and they continue to contaminate the water and soil. They include all sorts of pesticides. According to Marion Nestle, "In 2003, researchers compared the levels of pesticide 'excretion products' in the urine of preschool children who were fed organic or conventional diets. The urine of those fed conventional foods contained six times as many pesticide residues as were found in the urine of children who ate organics." [10]

THE ORGANIC OPTION

What does organic mean? The organic movement started in the 1960s and '70s as reaction to the environmental and health effects of chemical fertilizers and pesticides. The problem is that there is no way to really assess the long-term damage of exposure to chemical fertilizers and pesticides. Moreover, some studies indicate that "… levels of vitamin C and iron seem to be greater in some organically grown crops." [11] If you ask me, there's no reason not to eat organic fruits and vegetables whenever possible.

Organic farmers advocate maintaining a sustainable environment. Organic foods must be grown or produced without chemical pesticides and fertilizers, and not be genetically modified, irradiated, or cloned. The U.S. Department of Agriculture (USDA), which regulates certification of organic products, requires that they contain 95% organic ingredients. According to the USDA, "Organic food is produced without using most conventional pesticides; fertilizers made with synthetic ingredients or sewage sludge; bioengineering; or ionizing radiation." [12] (Organic livestock is raised without the use of antibiotics or growth hormones.)

In principle, the organic movement is a good thing, but this, too, has become big business. Since 2002, sales of organic fruit and vegetables have grown rapidly. Currently, the organic food market is worth almost $31 billion. [13] Large-scale organic farms are managing thousands of acres, so chances are there are still issues of soil depletion because of the need to produce large quantities of food.

In addition, these big farms need to reach their markets, which, as the farms become more successful, are farther and farther away from the fields where the produce is grown. Transporting the goods becomes a larger environmental factor. For instance, you'll see organic fruits shipped or flown from faraway countries. While it's great that we are able to buy organic foods in any season, it's not great that we are adding to carbon emissions that are presumably widening the hole in the ozone layer. And because these farming operations can be so large-scale, it's not clear that the conditions are healthy for laborers. As a 2011 scandal involving *e. coli*-infected organic spinach shows, cross-contamination of the soil is a real hazard.

It's a fact that organic foods generally cost more than non-organic, so, especially if you're on a budget, you may be faced with having to choose between the two. When it comes to produce, my rule of thumb is to purchase the non-organic option that has a thick skin or grows above ground. By peeling off the skin, I'm removing some of the pesticides in the foods. Similarly, foods that grow underground tend to have been exposed to pesticides concentrated in the soil. Some good choices include bananas, pineapple, nuts (not peanuts), most citrus fruits, avocados, butternut and acorn squash. I try to never compromise when it comes to milk, eggs, meat, and poultry. If organic cheese is not an option, I buy brands that carry the designation "DOP" or "AOC" (*appellation d'origine controlée*), which means the makers have followed traditional production methods.

We should all purchase organic foods whenever we can, though, because we are casting a vote for them with every dollar we spend. We are telling the food companies and the government that we will not tolerate the use of pesticides, fertilizers, and other harmful chemicals. Ultimately, as the demand for organic foods increases and there is more competition in the marketplace, their prices will come down.

So organic produce is good, but it's a first step. It's best to buy local produce because you are getting the food when it is at its maximum nutrient level. The minute you harvest a fruit or vegetable, it starts losing nutrients. Foods produced locally are responsible for less pollution because they are not traveling as far. Often, the local farms are small, so even though they may not have organic certification, which is very expensive, they tend to follow organic principles or use integrated pest management techniques, which are friendlier on the environment (and less depleting of the soil). It's important to ask what sort of practices the farm whose food you are buying is following.

THE BEST AND WORST FRUITS AND VEGETABLES TO EAT

The Environmental Working Group publishes a list of the best (those with lowest levels of pesticides) and worst (those with highest levels of pesticides) fruits and vegetables to eat. Here's its 2012 list:

SOURCE: WWW.EWG.ORG/FOODNEWS/SUMMARY

BEST

The foods that are the **lowest in pesticides** are the following:

- Onions
- Sweet corn
- Pineapples
- Avocados
- Cabbage
- Sweet peas
- Asparagus
- Mangos
- Eggplant
- Kiwis
- Cantaloupes (domestic - U.S.)
- Sweet potatoes
- Grapefruit
- Watermelons
- Mushrooms

WORST

The foods that are the **highest in pesticides** are the following:

- Apples
- Celery
- Bell peppers
- Peaches
- Strawberries
- Nectarines (imported)
- Grapes (imported)
- Spinach
- Lettuce
- Cucumbers
- Blueberries (domestic)
- Potatoes
- Kale
- Collard greens

THE LOCAL FOOD MOVEMENT

This is what prompted the development of the local food movement. The definition of what is "local" is essentially what you make of it — it can be 25, 50, or 100 miles but in my experience, local usually means produce grown no farther than 100 miles from where you bought it. Eating locally grown foods helps support local economies, cuts down on food miles, and promotes fresh, seasonal produce. Because the farms are nearby, the food tastes better — naturally, it's fresher! When foods are coming across the country or from other countries, they are picked when they aren't fully ripened and then shipped. When you get a bagged salad (organic or not) from the supermarket shelf, it was harvested 2-3 weeks before. Also, chemicals are needed to maintain freshness in the bag.

Another problem with commercial fruit and vegetable production is that farmers are increasingly focusing on the best-selling crops. As a result, agricultural diversity is decreasing year after year. It's interesting to note that, according to a United Nations study done in 2004 and reported in *Sustaining Life: How Human Health Depends on Biodiversity*, "Of all the myriad species of plants or animals whose products can be useful to humans, agriculture directly uses only a few hundred. Among these, just eighty crop plants and fifty animal species provide most of the world's food. According to the U.N.'s Food and Agriculture Organization, a total of only twelve plant species provide approximately 75 percent of our total food supply, and only fifteen animal, mammal, and bird species make up more than 90 percent of global domestic livestock production."[14] So we rely on fewer plants and animals for our nutrition.

The best thing about fruits and vegetables is that they are pretty much all healthy for us. It makes a big difference to our diet and health when we incorporate lots of fruits and vegetables. But even here it is important to find balance and moderation. The good thing is that even if you eat a vegetable or fruit in excess, it is not likely to do as much damage to your health as a soda or Twinkies ™. Nonetheless, in general, it is best not to eat too many starchy vegetables such as potatoes or corn because these contain a lot of simple sugars that are digested quickly (more on this later). Also, nightshade vegetables such as eggplants, peppers, potatoes, and tomatoes can cause inflammation, so it is best to avoid eating too much of these, or at least buffer them with some good-quality dairy products such as yogurt or cheese. Lemons, oranges, and grapefruit are rich in vitamin C, so are particularly good for fighting colds. Some of my personal favorites are onions, garlic, sweet potatoes, squash, asparagus, mushrooms, chard, cauliflower, cabbage, carrots, beets, avocados, apples, pears, and berries.

These are general comments, and foods react differently with different people, so it is best to see how you feel when you eat a specific food. If there is a food that you really don't want to eat, it probably means that it is not healthful to you at this point in time. I recently told a client that she would benefit from soups and porridges and she commented on how funny it was that I said that because she had been craving rice porridge recently.

Meat and Poultry

WE GET A LOT OF MIXED MESSAGES ABOUT MEAT: eat it, don't eat it, eat only white meat, eat only red meat…. Some people do very well without meat and some people don't. I am one of those who need meat. A few years ago, after a trip to Argentina during which I felt I had eaten all the cows on the Pampas, I decided to do a cleanse. I signed up for a two-day raw juice cleanse. After day one, I was on the couch shivering and exhausted. I decided that there are better ways to detox my body than deprive it of nutrients that it needs. My husband did the same cleanse and was fine, and he can do very well without eating meat. So, it really is an individual decision. I eat grass-fed red meat once or twice a week and eat poultry, eggs, fish, or grains the rest of the time. However, what works for me might not necessarily work for you. See how your body feels, as it is the best judge.

If you do eat meat, it's important to understand a few things about how it is raised. The problem with meat and poultry today is that they have become so over-produced that it is very difficult to ascertain exactly how healthy they are. Sometimes it seems as though we are eating more hormones and antibiotics than food. Frankly, the way most meat and poultry are raised today is inhumane.

The ideal mode of raising beef and lamb is for these animals to be grass-fed. Grass-fed animals eat nothing but their mother's milk, grass, and cut hay. Today, however, most cows are raised in overcrowded feedlots and pumped with hormones that create the most marketable products, i.e., meatier animals, at the least cost. Excessive hormones in cows, like excessive hormones in humans, are not healthy and can cause hormone imbalances of all sorts. Just as a human mother is not meant to nurse her baby past the age of five, a cow is not meant to produce milk continuously until old age. When cows are fed hormones to increase milk production, they risk getting mastitis – an infection in the breast tissue – for which they need antibiotics.

Cows also have to be given antibiotics because they are not meant to eat grains. When corn is fed to cows it causes severe indigestion, which weakens their immune systems, and the antibiotics are given to combat the resulting illnesses. As Marion Nestle notes in her book *What to Eat*, "The digestive systems of cows and sheep are set up to handle grass. The rumen in the stomach works like a fermentation vat; it contains vast numbers of bacteria that convert chewed-up grass and hay into nutrients (something we cannot do). The animals use these nutrients to grow and make meat. Ruminants are not meant to handle the more concentrated fats, proteins and carbohydrates in soybeans and corn. Eating concentrated feed made from corn and soybeans makes cattle grow faster and fatter, but it alters the mix of bacteria in their rumens. This gives them the equivalent of cow indigestion; the animals are not as healthy and need antibiotic treatment more frequently."[15] This is why it is crucial to eat grass-fed beef and lamb.

Similarly, chickens are meant to be wandering around eating grubs and worms and some grain (such as millet). Often, they are raised in crowded conditions on an all-grain diet and given antibiotics. And so the story goes with pork. The pigs live in crowded pens; they are force-fed genetically modified corn and soy (more on that later) and pumped with antibiotics in case they get sick.

This is why it is really important to read the labels on your meat products and know where your meat comes from! There are many different labels for meat and poultry products, "Natural" or "Certified Humane" for example, but these don't mean anything. The most important information to know is whether or not the animals were fed antibiotics or hormones, and whether they are grass-fed, in the case of cattle and sheep, or raised free-range in the case of poultry. The label should say this; if it doesn't, then the animals were not grass-fed or free-range. Animals should have access to pasture, sun, and enough land for exercise, and grazing should be done in a way that doesn't degrade the land. As I mentioned before, everything around us has energy and when organisms are raised with negative energy, that is what we get in return.

MEATS TO CHOOSE

These are the meats I choose when I am cooking, but it is important to do your research and find the best sources based on where you are located:

- Antibiotic-free pork with outdoor access
- Free-range poultry (and eggs)
- Grass-fed beef and lamb
- Heritage breeds of beef, poultry, turkey, and pork

Fish

THERE ARE MANY FACTORS I TAKE INTO ACCOUNT WHEN I CHOOSE FISH. First of all, is the fish wild? I prefer wild fish that are sustainably caught. Second, if I choose a farmed fish, is it sustainably farmed? There are some fish that I just stay away from: farmed salmon, tuna, and swordfish. I tend to prefer Pacific halibut, wild salmon, wild shrimp, and sole. Of course, this really depends on where you live and what is available there, so I find it best to use a guide. If you have a good fish-monger, he should be able to tell you where the fish is from and how it is sourced.

Obviously, since fish are mainly caught in the wild, we can't control what the fish eat, so unless they are farm-raised, fish aren't organic. With fish, there are three main issues: too much mercury in their tissue from the ocean pollution, a scarcity of certain species as a result of overfishing and destruction of natural habitats, and the health risks involved in eating farmed fish.

MERCURY

Mercury occurs naturally in the environment and is also the product of industrial pollution. When released, it contaminates the air and water. When it comes in contact with water, it is converted to methylmercury. Fish absorb methylmercury and over time it can build up to very toxic levels in their bodies. The larger the fish, the higher the levels of toxic chemicals they are likely to have accumulated because they have been exposed to methylmercury for longer periods than younger species, and because the larger fish are likely to have eaten smaller methylmer-cury-exposed fish.

If we eat fish containing high levels of mercury, such as shark, tuna, swordfish, dolphin (mahi-mahi), king mackerel, or tilefish, the mercury accumulates in our bodies, too, and we are susceptible to mercury poisoning, which has been shown to affect the brain and nervous system. A most severe form of mercury poisoning is Minamata disease, named after the island in Japan where it was discovered in the 1956. People who had the neurological disease, apparently caused by the mercury pollution from a nearby chemical factory, suffered blindness, deafness, loss of coordination, and impaired mental function.

OVERFISHING

Overfishing has become a serious problem, especially in Europe. The natural population of many fish is in steep decline. According to a 2005 Food and Agriculture Organization (FAO) report, about 52% of fish stocks are fully exploited, 24% are overly exploited, and 21% are moderately exploited.[16] Cod is one of those fish.

As journalist Taras Grescoe notes in his book, *Bottomfeeders: How to Eat Ethically in a World of Vanishing Seafood*, "Cod in particular were the apex predators in [Nova Scotia]. They prowled the gullies offshore in dense shoals, using their powerful mouths to suck up free-swimming lobster larvae, sea urchins, and even full-grown crustaceans. But the cod were fished to collapse in the early 1990s. With the cod gone, stocks of lobsters and other low-in-the-food-chain species exploded. It is a story that has been repeated throughout the Atlantic...." [17] By exploiting our resources to such an extent, we create an imbalance in the environment.

In other instances, trawlers drag large wire nets along the sea floor, completely destroying the natural environment. Grescoe notes, "The monkfish's bottom-dwelling ways were once its best defense against fishermen. Long ago, however, technology caught up with it.... In U.S. waters most monkfish are caught with bottom-trawls, cone-shaped nets that rake the sea bottom at speeds of two to six knots.... In areas that once provided safe haven for bottom-feeders, canyon-busters, tickler chains, and rockhoppers (heavy steel and rubber wheels that can jump huge boulders) scour every cranny in the seafloor.... A trawl's bottom edge dislodges the fish from their lairs and knocks them into the net, raising choking sand clouds as it carves gouges into the seabed." [18]

FISH FARMING

Fish farming came about so that large food companies could provide cheap food. Fish farming is not a great method of producing fish because most of the time it is similar to factory-farmed meat and poultry. One of the few exceptions is tilapia, where farming has been shown to actually have beneficial results because the nutrient-rich fish water is used to feed plants. Farmed rainbow trout and arctic char are other good options. Arctic char is quite similar to salmon, so it is a good substitute if wild salmon is not available. There are other fish that can be sustainably farmed and, again, it is important to do your research to find healthy fish.

With fish like salmon and shrimp, it's an entirely different story. Farmed salmon and shrimp are like cattle or chickens in feedlots. They swim in pools of waste and chemicals, such as antibiotics, dyes, and pesticides. Farmed salmon are treated with pesticides, and they eat fish-meal pellets containing artificial colors, parts of fish and other animals, and binders and thickeners made from soybeans that could be genetically modified. Farmed salmon contain significantly higher levels of PCBs, DDT, dioxins, pesticides, mercury, and other carcinogens that most wild salmon do because of the fish meal they eat.

Salmon, in particular, are fed a diet that contains everything but the tiny shrimp called krill, which is what they are supposed to be eating. In addition, because they are in such close confinement, they often get sea lice for which they need to be treated with antibiotics. Also, the farmed fish often escape and the sea lice contaminate the wild fish population. Finally, because farmed fish don't have that bright red color salmon is meant to have, they are given dyes to boost their color.

Now, it is sometimes possible to find organic farmed salmon. But they are still farmed and fed a diet of organic corn and soy. As Taras Grescoe notes in his book, "Salmon farms are offshore feedlots for converting brown pellets into edible, pink-hued flesh…. The biggest question mark hovers over ingredient number one on the feed bags: crude protein. In the wild, salmon are top-of-the food chain predators, subsisting, at various times in their life cycle, on plankton, krill, squid and smaller fish. Industrial aquaculture, however has turned them into consumers of some of the nastier by-products of land animals. Salmon feed contains "poultry meal," an industrial product made from the intestines, undeveloped eggs, spray-dried blood, necks and feet of poultry – in the jargon of the trade, all the 'nonfood parts' left over after processing. Normally indigestible feathers are hydrolyzed to make a dusty powder called feather meal; chicken manure – a potentially rich source of tapeworms, salmonella and arsenic – is also a key ingredient in salmon feed…. Were it not for the artificial colorants, the flesh of farmed salmon would be an unappetizing gray, yellow, or khaki. In the wild, salmon owe their pink hue to krill and shrimp, which contain the organic pigments astaxanthin and canthaxanthin. In salmon farms, artificial versions, synthesized from algae or yeast, are added directly to the feed…. Artificial colorants are only the start. When bacteria sickens salmon, farmers add antibiotics and other medications directly to their feed to control the outbreak."[19] Frankly, the very thought of eating farmed salmon repulses me.

To add insult to injury, companies are now creating genetically modified salmon. According to the Center for Food Safety, the salmon has been developed by combining salmon growth hormone genes and antifreeze genes from an eelpout. As a result, the fish produce growth hormones all year-round, which cause them to grow at twice their normal rate. Not only does this harm the local wild fish populations, but one imagines, though no research has been done, that it would have a negative effect on those who eat it as well.

Fats

MACRONUTRIENTS ARE CONSIDERED THE BUILDING BLOCKS OF LIFE — they consist of carbohydrates, fats, and proteins. I don't like to think of the food I eat in terms of carbohydrates, fats, proteins (plus vitamins, and minerals) because I can't be bothered to count ounces, grams, and milligrams, and I know that I need some combination of all of them. Some days I will need more carbohydrates, other days more fats, and others more protein. I trust my body to tell me what it needs. I have also realized that when I don't eat whole foods, my body gets confused about what to eat and I end up making poor food choices.

One of the macronutrients that is extremely underrated, however, is fats. By maligning fats, medical professionals have wreaked havoc on people's health. I can't stress this too much: we need fats! Our bodies generally have not evolved all that far from those of our caveman ancestors and will store fat for those times when food supplies are scarce. So, when you deprive your body of fats (say, by eating a low-fat diet) your body will store whatever fat it has for the day when no food is available.

And that's the key: We don't need the bad unsaturated fats such as margarine and soybean oil; we need the good healthy saturated and monounsaturated fats such as butter, ghee, olive oil, and coconut oil. Every traditional culture from the Eskimos to the Masai, to the French and the Indonesians have used some form of saturated fats in their cuisine, whether it is fish oil, fat from meat, butter, or coconut oil. The problem is that the healthy fats aren't cheap, and food manufacturers seem to prefer to use the inexpensive stuff in their products.

Fats provide the highest concentration of energy of all nutrients. Among many important roles, fat moves vitamins throughout the body and is the largest reserve of stored energy available for activity. In addition, fat surrounds the vital internal organs and serves as a shock absorber; it insulates the body from extreme temperatures.[20] Some vitamins, such as vitamins A, D, E, and K, are only absorbable when consumed with fats; they are found in foods that contain fat and are best absorbed from these foods. A final, important role of fat is that it helps you feel full after a meal. If you don't feel full, your tendency will be to eat more, which is why so many low-fat diets fail and actually end up causing weight gain.

For cooking, you want to use healthy fats, such as olive oil, organic butter, ghee, coconut oil, and unrefined sesame oil. For salads, flaxseed and nut oils are good. Nuts, seeds, and avocados are also very healthy fats. The less refined or processed the oil is, the better. If canola oil weren't genetically modified, I would say that it is also a healthy fat because it is high in Omega-3 fatty acids (more on this below). But it is made from a genetically modified seed, so it is not the healthiest of oils to use. For high-heat cooking, I prefer to use ghee or grapeseed oil.

Corn and soybean oils are too high in Omega-6 fatty acids (as are safflower and sunflower oils) and are usually full of pesticides. They are derived from grains that are, most likely, genetically modified. It is also worthwhile to note that increasingly research is showing that the cause of many inflammatory diseases (diabetes, heart disease, and stroke, among others) is the imbalance between the polyunsaturated Omega-3 and Omega-6 fatty acids, and we are not getting enough Omega-3s.

Omega-3 fatty acids are incorporated into cells, making their membranes more fluid so they can communicate with one another; they help in developing the brain, are anti-inflammatory, and support blood circulation. Omega-3 fatty acids can be found in fish, flax seeds, walnuts, and leafy green vegetables.

TRANSFATS

The fats to avoid: transfats. Trans-fatty acids (transfats) result from hydrogenation or partial hydrogenation of vegetable oils. As Mary G. Enig notes in *Know Your*

GOOD FATS

These are the fats I like to use:

- Butter
- Coconut oil
- Ghee*
- Nut and flaxseed oils **
- Olive oil
- Unrefined sesame oil

* Ghee is clarified butter, in which the milk proteins have been boiled off. Ghee can be used by those who are lactose intolerant or allergic to dairy because it does not contain casein. Also, ghee has a very high smoke point so it can be used in high-heat cooking.

**These should be used for salads only and not for cooking.

Fats: the Complete Primer for Understanding the Nutrition of Fats, Oils and Cholesterol,
"Beginning in the 1950s, the food industry capitalized on its ability to turn the
domestically produced seed oils, which were plentiful, but not sufficiently marketable as liquid oils, into solid fats for the budding fast food industry and for the
expanding baking and snack food industry."[21] This process, called hydrogenation,
involves transforming liquid oils from polyunsaturated fats, primarily soybean oil,
into solid fats, giving the oil a longer shelf life. In partial hydrogenation, half of the
polyunsaturated fatty acids remain. Transfats have been shown to cause cancer,
heart disease, and other inflammatory conditions such as Alzheimer's. As Marion
Nestle notes, "Hydrogenation causes some of the hydrogens in unsaturated and
polyunsaturated fatty acids to flip abnormally from the same side of the carbon chain
(in Latin, *cis*) to the opposite side (*trans*).... But the change to trans causes unsaturated fatty acids to stiffen. They behave a lot like saturated fatty acids in the body,
where they can raise cholesterol and increase the risk of heart disease."[22] Better to
use a little of the real stuff than to use these scientifically altered versions of fats.

Milk

I FIRST MOVED TO THE UNITED STATES WHEN I WAS EIGHT YEARS OLD. I have a clear
recollection of spending a weekend at a farm in Pennsylvania with my parents.
While there, I drank glass after glass of milk. The milk tasted delicious. In France,
where I'd lived previously, only nursing babies drank milk. It is mainly in America
that there is such a large consumption of milk. And that's just the problem
nowadays. People drink too much milk.

Milk is another controversial and confusing product. On the one hand, we are
sent the message to drink milk every day for strong bones. On the other hand, we
do not have a biological need for milk after the age of five. I mean, as my teacher Dr.
Annemarie Colbin, used to say, "How many adult cows, elephants, and giraffes do
you see drinking milk?" The other thing is that often we are allergic to it because the
lactase that enables digestion of milk is removed from the milk during processing.

Milk is processed in different ways: homogenization, ultra-pasteurization,
and pasteurization. Homogenization blends the milk at high speed so the cream
doesn't separate from the milk. This is apparently done to create a creamier-
looking product, not one with an added health advantage. In fact, the process of
homogenization tends to destroy many of the nutrients in the milk.

Ultra-pasteurized milk has been heated to 280°F for 2 seconds to kill the
bacteria. Similarly, pasteurized milk is heated to 145°F for a half-hour or 161°F

for 15 minutes, a process that eradicates most bacteria. According to Sally Fallon, nutrition researcher and author of *Nourishing Traditions*, the heat of pasteurization "alters milk's amino acids lysine and tyrosine, making the whole complex of proteins less available [sic]; it promotes rancidity of unsaturated fatty acids and destruction of vitamins…. Pasteurization reduces the availability of milk's mineral components, such as calcium, chloride, magnesium, phosphorus, potassium, sodium and sulfur, as well as many trace minerals."[23]

Conventionally processed milk contains hormones and antibiotics. According to Robyn O'Brien, author of *The Unhealthy Truth*, as of 1998, roughly 30% of all cows in the U.S. were being injected with the artificial, genetically engineered growth hormone called recombinant Bovine Growth Hormone (rBGH).[24] The hormone increases cows' milk production and also requires increased use of antibiotics because it creates disorders of the uterus, cystic ovaries, and mastitis in cows. So, when choosing milk, you should choose organic, non-homogenized, or raw milk. Most traditional cuisines use only a small amount of dairy, so it is generally not a main source of nutrition. This is, in my view, the best way to treat milk. It was used particularly in colder climates where green vegetables were hard to come by in winter, such as Northern Europe and Russia.

MILK SUBSTITUTES

Some good substitutes for milk are:

- Almond milk (unsweetened)
- Hazelnut milk
- Oat milk
- Rice milk

ORGANIC V. RAW MILK

Organic milk from grass-fed cows is rich in vitamins and minerals. It contains potassium, vitamins C and B, and is an important source of vitamins A and D. Grass-fed milk is rich in conjugated linoleic acid (CLA), an Omega-6 fatty acid that behaves like an Omega-3 fatty acid in the body, and which has been shown to prevent heart disease, fight cancer, and build lean muscle. Raw milk is often more digestible than pasteurized milk because it still contains all the enzymes necessary for proper digestion.

Sugar

I SEE MANY CHILDREN WHO GO FROM SUGAR RUSH TO SUGAR RUSH. They start the day with a sugary breakfast and are able to get enough energy to sustain them until mid-day, at which point they crash and snack on something containing more sugar. That rush keeps them going for another couple of hours, until they need more sugar to last them until the evening. I also find that sugar makes children very edgy and aggressive. The best thing to do is get rid of sugar altogether, or at least make it a rare treat and not a necessity. Sugar used to be used for medicinal purposes, as a sedative, tranquilizer, painkiller, and sleep inducer. There's been much discussion about whether or not sugar should be classed as a drug because its effects on the blood are so powerful and, many say, addictive. To make sugar, sugar cane is refined to a powder. In the process, all the vitamins, nutrients, and fiber in the sugar cane are removed and the remaining product is crystallized and then bleached. Unfortunately, today, sugar has become such a large part of our diet that it is highly addictive, high in calories, and low in nutrition.

In the body, sugar also wreaks havoc on our immune systems, by causing fluctuations in blood glucose levels. When a food contains fiber, the fiber slows the absorption of the food, and the blood glucose levels take longer to elevate and then lower. However, when a food is devoid of fiber, the glucose causes a spike in blood glucose levels followed by a sudden crash. When our bodies take in sugar, blood glucose levels increase and the pancreas starts to secrete (release) insulin in order to lower the blood glucose levels. When this happens frequently (say, from drinking too much soda, or overindulging in cookies, chocolate bars, or white bread and pasta) the pancreas starts to lose its ability to regulate blood sugar levels. Over time, this condition can become diabetes or hypoglycemia. In simple terms, diabetes occurs when the blood sugar doesn't return to its normal level, resulting in the need for chemical insulin to bring the sugar back down. In contrast, hypoglycemia means that the blood sugar drops too far below its normal level because too much insulin is released. In order to elevate the blood sugar to normal levels, a person suffering from hypoglycemia needs to eat something sweet. Hypoglycemia can create fatigue, restlessness, irritability, confusion, and poor memory, as well as hunger, dizziness, and "brain fog."

In addition, when we eat too much sugar, the pancreas floods the bloodstream with other hormones to bring the blood sugar down to normal levels. In this way, sugar also disrupts the body's immune, endocrine, and nervous systems. As insulin levels go up, growth hormones are prevented from being released, which subsequently weakens the immune system. Fluctuations in blood sugar also affect

SUGARS AND SWEETENERS TO USE

Here are sweeteners I use. Keep in mind that honey is a concentrated sweetener so it is best used sparingly. Nevertheless, I find it very comforting and like to use it when I have trouble sleeping, or when I have a cold or sore throat.

- Barley malt
- Brown rice syrup
- Coconut palm sugar
- Date sugar
- Honey
- Maple syrup and sugar
- Palm sugar

the brain. They can cause hyperactivity and restlessness, lack of concentration, mood swings, low energy, depression, and violent tendencies. The digestion of sugar also depletes the body of other important minerals. In particular, when you consume white sugar, B vitamins are taken from other parts of the body to digest the sugar, as are calcium, phosphorus, and iron. These are all important minerals that the body needs to grow and remain healthy.

High-fructose corn syrup (HFCS) is even worse than regular, refined sugar because research has shown that large amounts of fructose stimulate the liver's ability to make fat. Fructose has been shown to trigger hunger, whereas glucose will signal the brain to stop eating. HFCS is much cheaper than regular sugar, which is why it is now used in so many processed foods.

NATURAL SUBSTITUTES

Agave nectar is a natural sweetener made of plant extracts that is said to have originated in Latin America. Due to the increased demand for agave nectar, the way it is processed has changed so much that in its final formulation it now resembles high-fructose corn syrup. Stevia is another sugar substitute that one can now find in most health food stores. Although scientists are still researching the benefits and health risks of stevia, the way it is transformed from a plant to a fine white powder would seem to indicate that it undergoes extensive processing.

ARTIFICIAL SWEETENERS

Artificial sweeteners are even more unhealthful than refined sugars. They are made with chemicals that can cause serious harm to the body, and they trick the body in such a way that invariably people who consume them end up with an increased appetite. First the chemicals: It happens that these artificial sugars contain formaldehyde and DDT, among others. Second, when you eat artificial sugars, your body thinks that food is coming, so your digestive system starts preparing for the arrival of food. The problem is that there is no food to digest, but your pancreas starts secreting insulin, which causes your blood sugar to drop, and, in turn, makes you feel hungry and sluggish.

Wheat Products

WHEAT HAS BECOME A CONTROVERSIAL GRAIN RECENTLY. Wheat contains a protein called gluten, which seems to be causing immune responses in many people — from an inability to digest gluten to a chronic condition known as celiac disease, which is thought to affect 1 in 33 people. Found in wheat, rye, barley, and sometimes oats, gluten is what makes breads and pastas chewy.

Gluten intolerances have become much more prevalent in recent years. No one really knows why, but one of the reasons may be that we are no longer consuming the same types of wheat that our ancestors consumed. Another reason may be that, because people are consuming more refined grain products (such as white flour), they may have reduced ability to digest gluten, which is found in the endosperm of seeds and is what is left when you have removed the bran and germ of the wheat. It might also be because much of the wheat produced today is genetically modified. A final consideration is that we may just know how to better diagnose the problem when people show the symptoms.

When someone with celiac disease consumes gluten-containing foods, antibodies that protect intestinal microvilli are attacked. As a result, nutrient absorption is impaired. People may suffer from diarrhea, weight loss, malnutrition, migraines, infertility, and osteoporosis, among other conditions.

GLUTEN-FREE GRAINS AND FLOURS I LIKE TO USE

People who have celiac disease or intolerance to gluten need to eliminate all gluten-containing foods from their diets. The best grains to use instead of wheat, rye, and barley are:

- Brown rice
- Buckwheat (related to rhubarb and not wheat)
- Gluten-free oats
- Millet
- Non-GMO corn
- Quinoa

I am not intolerant to gluten, but I like to use brown rice pasta and brown rice or other whole grains, such as barley, millet, quinoa, amaranth, and farro. Here are the flours:

- Barley flour*
- Chickpea flour
- Hazelnut flour
- Oat flour*
- Quinoa flour
- Rice flour

* While barley and oat flour are not gluten-free, they are better to use than refined white flour because they are made with whole grains.

REFINED WHITE WHEAT FLOUR

Refined white wheat flour has an effect on the body similar to that of sugar because it is stripped of its fiber content and, therefore, causes fluctuations in blood sugar levels, as I described above. In the case of wheat, the flour is refined and processed to make white flour, which is used in baking breads, cookies, cereals, and more. As nutrition expert Marion Nestle notes, "The milling of whole grains makes the calories go up and everything else go down. White flour has more calories than whole-wheat flour because it is more concentrated; it has lost its fibrous bran, which does not weigh much and has hardly any calories (although it has plenty of nutrients). When the bran is taken away, the vitamins and minerals go away with it (and make great animal feed)."[25]

When we eat refined white flour products we are essentially eating sugar. Since there is no fiber, vitamins, or minerals in the refined wheat, we speed up the glucose release of the food. When too much glucose is released too quickly, blood sugar goes up because the pancreas makes too much insulin, and then we feel hungry again. It is worthwhile to note that most traditional cultures have some form of whole grain at their root: Asians use rice, Eastern Europeans use kasha/buckwheat, Middle Easterners use millet or couscous, the Scottish use oats, Southern Europeans use wheat, Peruvians use quinoa. The key difference is that traditional cultures consumed these grains whole and unrefined.

Corn and Soy

I NEVER KNOW HOW TO CATEGORIZE CORN AND SOY because nowadays they end up falling into so many foods. I'm not even sure whether they are foods anymore. In a classic example of a good government policy gone bad, in addition to wheat, corn and soy became popular when the U.S. government began to implement a cheap-food policy. So now there is so much corn and soy that manufacturers try to put it everywhere. As author Michael Pollan notes, "Why corn and soy? Because these two plants are among nature's most efficient transformers of sunlight and chemical fertilizer into carbohydrate energy (in the case of corn) and fat and protein (in the case of soy…)."[26] According to the USDA's National Agricultural Statistical Services, "U.S. farmers produced the largest corn and soybean crops on record in 2009."[27] Corn is found in cornstarch and high-fructose corn syrup. Soy is found in margarine and other vegetables oils or transfats, or as soy lecithin, a binder in many foods.

The problem is that corn and soy are often genetically modified and full of pesticides. (Below, I address some of the perils of genetically modified foods.)

In order to put these foods everywhere, they have to be refined and processed to such an extent that they are unrecognizable. Corn, for instance, is now used as a sugar. As you can imagine, in order to go from corn to high-fructose corn syrup, the corn has to undergo a lot of processing.

SOY

Soy is traditionally an Asian food. But, in Asia, it is used as a condiment and is generally fermented (miso, tempeh, and natto are all made from fermented soy). It is only in recent times that someone decided to use soy in everything from milk to processed foods. And the problem with this is that our bodies don't know what to make of these things that at one point were whole foods but now are not.

Recent studies have shown that too much soy can disrupt the function of the thyroid and prevent the proper absorption of protein. Moreover, soy contains phytoestrogens, which are structurally similar to estrogen and have been implicated in problems with sexual differentiation, breast cancer and endometric diseases. As Sally Fallon notes in her book *Nourishing Traditions*, "Soybeans are high in phytates and contain potent enzyme inhibitors that are only deactivated by fermentation and not by ordinary cooking. These inhibitors can lead to protein assimilation problems in those who consume unfermented soy products frequently…. Phytoestrogens found in soy foods, although touted as panaceas for heart disease, cancer, and osteoporosis, are potent endocrine disruptors as well as goitrogens – substances that depress thyroid function."[28] So soy is best approached with caution. I stick to the fermented kind and limit my intake of the non-fermented type to organic tofu and edamame.

Genetic Modification

IN NATURE, PLANTS AND ANIMALS CREATE NEW SPECIES when their genes combine with those of other plants and animals. This process has gone on for millions of years and this is how species change and develop over time. It is also how species of plants and animals adjust to evolving environmental conditions. In contrast, genetic modification is a process whereby the genes of one species of plant or animal are inserted into the genes of another in order to give that plant or animal certain positive traits. Genetic modification is different from what happens in nature because it cuts across species, mixing the genes of plants and animals.

In his book *Seeds of Deception: Exposing Industry and Government Lies About the Safety of the Genetically Engineered Foods You're Eating*, Jeffrey Smith notes that the

main problem with genetic modification (GM) is that it can have many unintended consequences on organisms. This is because genes from GM food products create proteins that aren't usually created by those food products. In effect, no one knows what reaction the insertion of a foreign gene into an organism will cause. Smith notes several problems associated with the insertion of a foreign gene into a body: Genes inserted into crops can create inadvertent proteins; no one knows the effect of other elements on these new proteins; the process of inserting new genes can damage the native genes; or a native gene can be disabled.[29] In effect, it appears that the foremost problem with genetic modification is that no one knows what happens when these newly created genes interact with our own genes.

Organisms are not simple machines in which what goes in is what comes out. On the contrary, there are many varied reactions to the same inputs and no one can clearly determine what those reactions will be. This is the problem with genetic modification: It often causes many other reactions that were not meant (or known) to happen.

Specifically, GM foods seem to cause severe allergies, antibiotic resistance, and weakened immune systems. These foods are said to cause allergic reactions because crossing genes from one species to another creates allergens. Also, in the process of genetic modification, allergenic foods (such as nuts, in particular) may be used, thereby causing allergic reactions in those who consume those foods. Moreover, GM foods can also cause antibiotic resistance because genes which are resistant to antibiotics are inserted into the cell's nuclei. These genes are used to help determine whether the host organism has accepted the GM genes. Finally, research has shown that GM foods can cause weakened immune systems and lead to the growth of tumors.

In addition to the foreign genes inserted into a plant or animal, scientists also insert another gene called an Antibiotic Marker Gene which is attracted to the foreign gene. The Antibiotic Marker Gene helps scientists determine which of the cells now have the foreign gene within their DNA. It also will prevent the cell from being affected by antibiotics. As a result, these Antibiotic Marker Genes can start spreading around the body and lead to general, widespread antibiotic resistance.[30]

My personal view on genetic modification is that I don't really want scientists creating what I eat in a laboratory. I would much rather trust nature and the millions of years of natural processes that have worked for many people until now. When I shop, I am careful to look for information on food labels that guarantees that no GM ingredients have been used, and you should, too.

cookhealthy

Follow the Recipes

WE TEND TO UNDERESTIMATE the extent to which a person's food choices can have a significant impact on his or her health. I think we have come to rely too heavily on the notion that western medicine will cure us of all our ills, without accepting that we also have a responsibility, even a duty, to ourselves. We have to think of our body as a car; if we want it to function properly, we need to service it regularly. We cannot think we can drive it into the ground and then expect a mechanic to fix everything. This is why it is so important to make food choices that impact our health in a positive way.

In an extensive study done in the 1930s, a dentist named Weston A. Price visited a number of traditional communities including the Eskimo of Alaska, Native Americans, and remote mountain communities in Switzerland to assess the extent to which the pervasiveness of western foods had affected the dental health of the population. In his book, *Nutrition and Physical Degeneration*, he notes, "A critical examination of these groups revealed a high immunity to many of our serious affections [sic] so long as they were sufficiently isolated from our modern civilization and living in accordance with the nutritional programs which were directed by the accumulated wisdom of the group. In every instance where individuals of the same racial stocks who had lost this isolation and who had adopted the foods and habits of our modern civilization were examined, there was an early loss of the high immunity characteristics of the isolated group."[31] In

other words, wherever western food has been introduced, lowered immunity and illness has followed.

And as Michael Pollan writes in *Food Rules: An Eater's Manual*, "We know there is a deep reservoir of food wisdom out there, or else humans would not have survived and prospered to the extent we have. This dietary wisdom is the distillation of an evolutionary process involving many people in many places figuring out what keeps people healthy (and what doesn't), and passing that knowledge down in the form of food habits and combinations, manners and rules and taboos, and everyday and seasonal practices, as well as memorable sayings and adages."[32]

I wholeheartedly agree with Michael Pollan and firmly believe that traditional recipes all have some form of health benefits. Traditional recipes focus on whole, real foods and have an intrinsic balance. For instance, as I mentioned before, nightshade vegetables can be inflammatory because they contain alkaloids, which can deplete the body of minerals. In many traditional recipes – Eggplant Parmesan, Gratin Dauphinois (*see recipe on p. 215*), Tomato Sauce with Parmesan Cheese — nightshade vegetables are paired with dairy products to replenish the minerals. Similarly, many cuisines originating in warm climates incorporate ingredients that have antibacterial properties, such as coconut milk and oil, garlic, ginger, onions, and chiles. Our ancestors inherently knew which foods were vital to their health. This is why it is so important to respect their wisdom when nourishing ourselves.

I have witnessed this in my travels. Very often, I see similarities in otherwise vastly different culinary traditions and see that those cultures that maintain a traditional diet are much healthier than those who adopt refined and processed foods. For instance, as India has developed and the wealthier classes have gained access to Western goods and processed foods, there has been a simultaneous increase in diseases like diabetes, heart disease, and cancer.

I was fortunate to be raised around family who valued traditional home-cooked foods. I think that it is important to take time to prepare nourishing food for the family. I see the difference in my own children: when they eat junk food, they are distracted, aggressive, fall sick more easily; in contrast, when they eat home-cooked food, they can concentrate for longer periods of time and don't succumb as easily to colds or other illnesses going around school.

Homemade foods contain a special vitamin no other foods contain, what Elson M. Haas, refers to as "vitamin L" for love. As Haas notes, "In food, it is especially found in home-cooked or other meals where vitamin L is used consciously as an ingredient....This vitamin acts as the "universal" vitalizing energy. Vitamin L helps to catalyze all human functions and is particularly important to heart function and the circulation of warmth and joy.[33] "Homemade foods naturally contain vitamin L because they have been made with the positive intention of nourishing one's family, as well as the positive energy to create something that is healthy.

Healthy Traditions

BEFORE I SHARE SOME OF THE RECIPES I LOVE, let me give you some background. I was born to parents of German heritage and raised in the South of France, a part of the world where food in all its Mediterranean glory is taken very seriously. I was taught about the significance of eating home-cooked foods in season. I think Mediterranean cuisine is one of my favorite cuisines because it is so flavorful yet not overpowering. The cuisine uses many vegetables, combined with a little bit of protein, mainly fish. Mediterranean cuisine is very simple and yet so healthy and delicious.

Many of the vegetables used in Mediterranean cuisine – eggplants, tomatoes, and peppers—are nightshade vegetables (because they grow at night). While these have many health benefits, they can also cause inflammation and have been shown to worsen pains such as arthritis. This is because they contain alkaloids, which tend to deplete the body of calcium. However, in many cuisines, such as Greek, Italian, and Indian, these are often paired with ingredients that reduce inflammation like cumin, turmeric, and cayenne, or that contain calcium, such as dairy or leafy green vegetables. In Greece and the Middle East, too, many meals are accompanied by a yogurt relish. In Italy, pasta with tomato sauce is topped with parmesan cheese. The bonus is that yogurt and hard, fermented cheeses like parmesan contain probiotics with a lot of beneficial bacteria, which strengthen the immune system. Like most, my childhood was influenced by many traditions. My maternal grandmother, who was Swiss-German, cooked with a lot of cream. The food was tasty and delicious but very rich. I remember my grandmother in her kitchen making her veal with mushrooms with tons of heavy cream. In Northern Europe, dishes such as Gratin Dauphinois or Vichyssoise soup are very common. Summers are short and winters are cold. The fat in cream and butter helps keep the body warm. The fat, which our bodies convert into fat cells, as I mentioned before, is important to insulate the body to keep it warm. Another reason is that animal fats, ghee, and butter are rich in vitamin A. Vitamin A helps us absorb vitamin D, which, in turn, is essential for calcium absorption. In those parts of the world where it is difficult to get vitamin D from the sun, vitamin A plays an even greater role in our health.

Cream and butter are a good source of vitamins that are unavailable from vegetables in winter. Also, because cows and goats eat grass and other leafy greens, we get those nutrients through them when we eat natural beef or lamb, in addition to consuming dairy products.

Another important food is sauerkraut, which is eaten primarily in winter. Sauerkraut is made of fermented cabbage, which is full of beneficial bacteria that strengthen the immune system. In Eastern Europe, where the climate is colder, there are more fermented foods.

I am fortunate to have had the opportunity to travel and, through my travels, have experienced many cuisines. As a young adult, I moved back to the United States from France to attend college and graduate school. After graduate school, I married an Indian man and we traveled to India every year. In the years since, in addition to living in the United States, we have lived in London and Singapore.

In addition to having lived many places, I have a rich cultural home life. The foods my husband grew up eating are a now part of our everyday meals. My husband is from Northern India, where there are Arab and Persian influences in the cuisine, making it very similar to the way the Mediterranean people eat. Their diet is rich in vegetables complemented by a lot of grains and beans, or mutton/lamb or poultry. Because cows are considered sacred in India, beef is not a part of the diet. However, dairy is used quite regularly in the form of yogurt and milk, as is ghee, a clarified butter in which the milk proteins have been boiled off. Also, there are many rice and legume dishes, which constitute a great source of protein.

While rice and legumes are a good source of protein, they are not a source of complete protein, as meat is, unless they are consumed together. Proteins are made up of 22 amino acids, 8 of which are considered essential because the body cannot

manufacture them. Animal products such as meat, poultry, and eggs are considered perfect proteins because they have all the amino acids the body requires. Rice and legumes (beans) have all eight amino acids, but within each group, two of them are in short supply; thus they are not complete proteins. However, when combined, rice and beans make up a complete protein. This is why most traditional cuisines feature a rice and bean dish.

In Southern India and many other Southeast Asian countries, the dietary reliance is more on fish and coconut as the primary source for fats and proteins. Also, coconut is a well-known antimicrobial, meaning it has properties that fight harmful microbes. Coconut oil is also a very healthy fat because, while it is a saturated fat, the fat in coconut oil is a medium-chain fatty acid, which means that it is easier to metabolize than long-chain fatty acids, and is composed of lauric acid, which has been shown to contain antiviral and antimicrobial properties. This is useful in countries with hot and humid weather, conditions where viruses and harmful microbes can flourish.

Where we used to live, in Asia, it is customary to combine sugar and chiles in dishes. Asian cuisines try to incorporate the five main flavors — sweet, sour, bitter, pungent, and salty — in their dishes, which is why you often see curries served with pickled vegetables or sauces with fermented shrimp paste, which may sound processed but can be made in the traditional way that involves whole ingredients. Incorporating the five flavors ensures that there is balance in the meal, which I will address in greater detail below.

As you would see elsewhere, the warmer climate of Southeast Asia influences what the people who live there eat. For instance, rice is the grain primarily eaten because the humidity helps the rice grow particularly well. There is less focus on meat products and more on fish because one can fish all year-round and because meat is a very warming food (often, the fish is salted and preserved so it can be used at a later time); it is customary to make an herb/spice paste, such as garlic-ginger or garlic-ginger-onion, which serves to flavor the oil, to slow the degradation of the oil during cooking, and to eliminate bacteria in the food (garlic, onions, and ginger are great antimicrobial herbs).

The differences in cuisines between colder and warmer countries can also be seen in the physiques of many of those people. For instance, many people from Northern Europe, Russia, and China have much larger bones and are generally bigger than people from Southeast Asia. This is thought to be because people in colder climates have to contend with more extreme weather conditions and, as such, likely need to be able to store more fat for winter. In some ways, our bodies have not evolved much from when man lived in caves and had to adjust to very specific environmental conditions. Our bodies have not adjusted to the 21st century, where you can get a papaya in the middle of winter in New York City, for example. This is why our bodies sometimes resist the changes we impose and why I stress that it is important to listen to what your body wants and needs.

SIMILARITIES AMONG TRADITIONAL CUISINES

What do I mean by "traditional" cuisines? I mean early diets. I mean eating habits that are very much the result of how people have evolved in their natural environments. Let me summarize the similarities among a few traditional cuisines.

- **Vegetables, legumes, and grains** are the focus of the meals. One exception to this is the Masai in Africa who eat primarily the milk, blood and meat of cattle, and the Eskimo, who also eat primarily fish and fish fats, along with some grains and berries.

- When there is a **protein** such as meat, fish, poultry, or eggs, it is usually in small quantities.

- **Sweeteners** come from fruit or sweet vegetables.

- **Fermented foods** are used such as sauerkraut, miso, kimchi, wine, yogurt, and salted fish. These are full of bacteria that boost the immune system (probiotics).

- **Healthy, unrefined fats** such as olive, coconut, or sesame oils, or ghee and butter are used.

- **Raw foods,** usually in the form of salads or pickled vegetables, are incorporated into meals. Raw foods are rich in nutrients and aid the digestive process. These are more common in warmer climates because they are cooling to the body. I do not think, however, that a diet of just raw foods is very healthy for the body because it is too cooling and there are some nutrients that can be absorbed only when the food is cooked.

Herbs and Spices

HERBS AND SPICES CAN ALSO HELP bring our bodies back into balance. This is why so many traditional cultures incorporate herbs in their cuisines. For instance, garlic, onions, and cayenne—all of which are antibacterial—are common in cuisines typical to warm countries. In Mediterranean cooking, you will find oregano, rosemary, thyme, garlic, and onions, among many other herbs. Asians use ginseng, mushrooms, ginger, and garlic. In Southeast Asia, there are turmeric, cayenne, and neem leaf, coming from a tree in the mahogany family native to the Indian subcontinent.

HEALING HERBS AND SPICES

Herbs have strong healing properties. As with many medicines, if they are not used properly, they will make you sick. If you have any questions, you should contact a medical professional before using. Here are some of my favorite herbs and spices.

ALOE VERA is a great herb for skin irritations, burns, and insect bites because it is very soothing and cooling.

ARNICA is an herb which, when used externally, can relieve pain and inflammation due to bruising and soreness. I use Arnica cream on my children for bumps or sprains. Arnica is never meant to be used internally unless it is in the form of a homeopathic remedy, so check with a medical professional before ingesting.

BURDOCK ROOT is a great digestive root. It helps reduce heat and inflammation in the liver and detoxifies poisons. It is also used to treat skin conditions like eczema and psoriasis, which are usually the result of a toxin on the inside trying to come out.

CALENDULA is used to remedy skin inflammations from infections or burns. Calendula can also be used internally to minimize inflammation of the digestive system as well as fungal infections.

CAYENNE PEPPER is a great blood tonic that helps stimulate blood flow. However, if there are any issues with inflammation, it is best to minimize the use of cayenne.

CHAMOMILE is another digestive herb. In addition to helping the digestive system and easing inflammation, it also calms the nervous system and can help alleviate stress and insomnia.

CINNAMON comes from the bark of the cinnamon tree. It's a great antimicrobial herb, and because it's warming, it's good for soothing a cold. Cinnamon is also said to aid in insulin regulation and blood clotting.

CUMIN is rich in vitamins A and C, both essential to the immune system. Cumin also contains iron, which helps with digestion and inflammation.

DANDELION is a bitter herb that is great for cleansing the liver and detoxifying the body. You can eat the leaves fresh or infused in teas.

ECHINACEA is an immune-strengthening herb that helps the body eliminate microbial infections, especially those in the respiratory tract. It is very useful in fighting colds and flu.

FENNEL is another great digestive herb that helps reduce gas and lower abdominal pain. It is also used to freshen the breath. In many Indian restaurants, there is usually a bowl of fennel seeds by the door.

GARLIC is an antimicrobial, antibacterial, and antifungal herb that helps fight colds, flu, and other infections. It has also been shown to lower blood pressure, act as a tonic for the heart, and help fight cancer.

GINGER is an anti-inflammatory herb that is used frequently to calm the digestive system, especially in cases of nausea, and to stimulate the digestive enzymes. Ginger also aids circulation in the body.

GINSENG ROOT is used frequently in the East as a general tonic. It is said to strengthen *qi* (the vital energy) and aid the digestive and immune systems, reduce fatigue, and slow aging.

KUZU ROOT is a root starch (similar to cornstarch or arrowroot) that is used as a tonic to help soothe the stomach and nerves. It is a great calming remedy for insomnia. My teacher, Dr. Annemarie Colbin, gave us a recipe with kuzu and apple juice as a remedy for insomnia, stress, and hyperactivity. I have found it to be very soothing and warming.

Here is my take on the recipe with blueberry juice instead of apple juice:

1 cup blueberry juice
1 cup blueberries (fresh or dried)
2 Tbsp. kuzu root starch
1 tsp. pure vanilla extract
1 Tbsp. tahini

Combine all ingredients, bring to a boil, and boil until thickened.

LEMON While not an herb, lemon has many healing properties. It is rich in vitamin C and so is great for fighting off colds and infections. It is also alkalizing and helps bring the body back in balance when it is too acidic (from too much sugar, caffeine, or alcohol). My first recourse for a sore throat or cough is a hot lemon juice with honey. I also drink a warm lemon juice with a pinch of sea salt and cayenne every morning before breakfast to "wake up" my digestive system. I make a glass of fresh-squeezed lemon juice with honey for my children every day to boost their immune systems.

NEEM is the herb of choice in India. It is said to reduce inflammation, fever, and itching. It is also used as an antibacterial and antimicrobial.

NETTLE is a bitter herb that has anti-inflammatory and digestive properties. It cleanses the blood and helps eliminate toxins from the kidneys. Like burdock root, it is helpful in relieving eczema and psoriasis.

OATS/OATSTRAW is both relaxing and anti-inflammatory.

ONION, like garlic, is an antioxidant and anti-microbial herb.

OREGANO is another antibacterial and antioxidant herb. It has also been shown to relieve coughing and to thin mucus. It stimulates appetite and detoxifies food.

PARSLEY is a great source of vitamin C. It is also a diuretic, so it helps the body eliminate excess water, and it eases digestive issues such as flatulence.

PEPPERCORNS help digestion because they stimulate the production of hydrochloric acid. They are also antibacterial and antioxidant.

PEPPERMINT is a great digestive herb that relaxes the muscles of the digestive system and stimulates the flow of bile and digestive juices. It is anti-inflammatory and can be used to treat colds, flu, and fevers. It is a very calming herb and helps reduce anxiety and stress.

ROSEMARY is an herb that stimulates the circulatory and nervous systems. It is useful for easing digestion when there is tension.

TEA TREE OIL is an antibacterial and antimicrobial oil that is useful to treat wounds and fungal infections. Tea tree oil should be used externally only. The tea tree is also known as the manuka tree, and manuka honey is said to have cancer-fighting properties.

THYME helps stimulate digestion. It can also be used internally and externally as an antiseptic.

TURMERIC is an anti-inflammatory root that helps reduce mucus, and treat inflammation-related conditions in the body.

Before We Eat

Food provides more than just physical nourishment; food provides us with emotional nourishment. This is why it is important to bless our food before we eat. Here is a blessing that I like from Iyanla Vanzant's book, *Every Day I Pray*:

Dear God:

Thank you for preparing this table before us.

Thank you for the bounty of the earth which nourishes our bodies.

Thank you for the abundance of your goodness, which sustains our lives, strengthening us to serve you more effectively.

Thank you for the hands that prepared this meal and for the joy of being able to share it.

For all we have received and all that is yet to come, God, we are thankful!

We are grateful! We are fulfilled!

And So It Is

General Recipe Notes

A few notes on the recipes. This is a selection of my favorite recipes from around the world, so it is by no means exhaustive. There are many recipes from different countries that I have yet to discover and they will hopefully be the subject of future publications.

1. The goal of these recipes is simplicity so they can be replicated at home without too much fuss.

2. I recommend using organic fruits, vegetables, grains, and beans; free-range poultry and eggs; grass-fed beef or lamb; sustainably raised fish; organic butter or ghee from grass-fed cows; cold-pressed oils, especially olive or sesame.

3. I generally use 1 tsp. of sea salt in each recipe, but I tend to prefer foods on the salty side so it is best if you experiment.

4. I prefer to use maple sugar for most of my recipes. Maple sugar is becoming easier to find, but if it's not available, you can use Sucanat. The less refined the sugar, the better.

5. I don't believe in low-fat or fat-free dairy products and would rather use a little bit of the full-fat stuff.

6. I also don't believe in frozen or canned foods because, as my teacher, Dr. Annemarie Colbin, once said, they are like dead foods, lacking in any energy. However, I do make an exception with frozen peas because it is so hard to find sweet fresh peas, and with crushed tomatoes from a glass jar (not canned).

Breakfast

PRIOR TO KELLOGG'S AND POST, many cultures ate traditional breakfasts of porridge, using the grain that was local to their regions. Usually these early morning repasts took the form of grain cooked in water or milk. Oats were (and remain) prevalent in Northern Europe; wheat in Southern Europe; kasha or buckwheat in Eastern Europe; rice in Asia; millet in the Middle East; and quinoa and corn in Latin America. These days, our definition of breakfast includes much more than porridge. We eat eggs, muffins, and fresh fruit, recipes for which you'll find in the pages that follow. I'm partial to porridges, so I've included some of my favorite recipes for these, too.

Fruit, Nut, and Maple Granola

I like to eat this with plain yogurt and fresh fruit. Yogurt is rich in probiotics to help support the immune system. Fruit are rich in vitamins and fiber, which helps the digestive system.

Serves 6

3	cups rolled oats
½	cup slivered raw almonds
¼	cup unsalted sesame seeds in the hull
½	cup unsweetened, shredded coconut
½	tsp. ground cinnamon
¼	cup unsalted butter, melted
½	cup grade B maple syrup
2	tsp. pure vanilla extract
½	cup raisins, dried blueberries, or currants, unsulfured and unsweetened

1. Preheat oven to 375°F.

2. Combine oats, almonds, sesame seeds, coconut, cinnamon, butter, syrup, and vanilla and spread in a thin layer across a large baking sheet.

3. Bake for 20-30 minutes until golden brown, stirring every 5-7 minutes.

4. Remove from oven and let cool. Stir in dried fruit.

5. Serve warm or cold. Can be stored in a tightly-sealed glass or plastic container for 3-4 weeks.

Traditional Swiss Muesli

My mother used to make muesli like this and it took me a long time to appreciate and enjoy it. Now I love it!

Serves 6

1   cup quick-cooking oats, soaked in water overnight

1   apple, grated

2   cups yogurt

½   cup slivered almonds

¼   cup raisins

1   cup seasonal fruit, cut up (berries, pineapple, and bananas are my favorites)

1. Drain and rinse oats.

2. Combine oats, apple, and yogurt in a medium bowl. Mix well.

3. Add almonds, raisins, and seasonal fruit.

Rhubarb and Strawberry Compote

This is a refreshing fruit compote for summer. It goes great with yogurt and granola.

Serves 6

3   cups rhubarb, stalks cleaned and trimmed, then cut into small pieces about ¾ in. long

¾   cups maple sugar or Sucanat

¼   cup water

½   lb. strawberries, hulled and quartered

     Fresh mint leaves, chopped

1. Combine rhubarb, maple sugar, and water in a large saucepan.

2. Bring to a boil and simmer for 5-7 minutes, until sugar has dissolved and rhubarb is soft.

3. Add strawberries. Stir well and add mint. Remove from heat immediately.

4. Cool to room temperature before serving.

Banana-Walnut Muffins

I love the strong banana flavor in these muffins and the crunch that the walnuts add. These muffins are a good gluten-free breakfast option.

Makes 12 muffins

3¼	cup millet flour
2	tsp. baking soda
½	tsp. cinnamon
½	tsp. sea salt
4	large eggs
2 ⅓	cups maple sugar
1	cup unsalted butter, melted
3	cups mashed bananas
¼	cup crème fraîche or sour cream
2	tsp. pure vanilla extract
1 ⅓	cups chopped walnuts (optional)

1. Preheat oven to 350°F. Butter a muffin tin or two 3x9-in. loaf pans and dust with flour.

2. Combine millet flour, baking soda, cinnamon, and salt in a medium bowl.

3. Put eggs and maple sugar in an electric mixer and beat until they are pale and thick. Add butter in a slow stream.

4. Add bananas, crème fraîche, and vanilla and mix well. Stir in the walnuts (if using).

5. Add dry ingredients and mix well.

6. Pour batter into muffin tin or loaf pans and bake 45 minutes-1 hour, until golden and a toothpick inserted in the center of a muffin or loaf comes out clean.

7. Cool on a rack.

Winter Fruit Compote

This tastes great with oatmeal or brown rice cereal.

Serves 6

2	sweet apples (Fuji or Gala), peeled and diced
2	pears (Bosc or Bartlett), peeled and diced
¼	cup orange juice
¼	cup water
2	cups unsweetened and unsulfured dried fruit such as apricots, apples, raisins, currants, cherries, or cranberries
½	vanilla bean, split length-wise, seeds scraped
1	star anise
6	strips orange zest

1. Combine apples, pears, orange juice, and water in a large pot.

2. Bring to a boil, reduce heat, and simmer until apples and pears are soft but not mushy. This should take 7-10 minutes, depending on how small the fruit is cut.

3. Add dried fruit, vanilla bean seeds, star anise, and orange zest and simmer for an additional 5 minutes.

4. Allow to cool a few minutes before serving.

Traditional French Spice Bread

This is one of my favorite breakfast breads because it reminds me of my childhood. What I love most is that it is not too sweet and tastes great spread with butter or cream cheese.

Makes one 9-in. loaf

3½	cups whole wheat flour
½	cup rye flour
2½	tsp. baking soda
1½	tsp. ground cinnamon
1½	tsp. ground ginger
½	tsp. sea salt
¼	tsp. ground nutmeg
¼	tsp. ground cloves
¼	tsp. freshly ground black pepper
¼	cup unsalted butter
1	large egg
1	cup honey
1	Tbsp. grated orange zest
1	cup water

1. Preheat oven to 350°F. Butter a 9-in. loaf pan and dust with flour.

2. Combine whole wheat flour, rye flour, baking soda, and spices in a medium bowl.

3. Put butter, egg, honey, and orange zest in an electric mixer and beat until thoroughly mixed.

4. Alternate adding water and dry ingredients.

5. Pour batter into loaf pan and bake 1 hour, until brown and a toothpick inserted in the center comes out clean.

6. Cool on a rack.

Everybody's Favorite Maple Bars

Everyone loves these because they are very moist and the coconut and oats give them an interesting texture. They can just as easily be served as dessert.

Makes 6 bars

½	cup maple sugar
½	cup grade B maple syrup
½	cup unsalted butter, melted
3	large eggs
⅔	cup whole-grain barley flour
1	cup unsweetened, shredded coconut
1	cup slow-cooking rolled oats
½	tsp. aluminum-free baking powder
1	tsp. pure vanilla extract

1. Preheat oven to 350°F.

2. Butter an 8x8-in. baking pan.

3. Whisk sugar, syrup, butter, eggs, flour, coconut, oats, baking powder, and vanilla thoroughly in a large bowl.

4. Pour mixture into baking pan and smooth with spatula.

5. Bake 30-35 minutes, until bars are brown and a knife inserted in the center comes out clean.

6. Let cool, then cut into 6 bars and serve.

Homemade Energy Bars

These are a great swap for the store-bought energy bars I used to eat because they don't contain too much sugar, have no preservatives, and are easy to make. This recipe makes a large tray, which you can keep in the refrigerator for up to 2 weeks.

Makes 20 small bars

¼   cup blanched, slivered almonds

1½   cups slow-cooking rolled oats

1   cup puffed brown rice cereal

1½   cups unsulfured dried apricots, chopped (you can also use dried apples)

1½   cups unsulfured dried currants (or dried blue-berries, cranberries, or raisins)

½   tsp. ground cinnamon

1   cup brown rice syrup (usually available at a specialty grocery store; if not, you can substitute barley malt)

½   cup grade B maple syrup

½   cup unsweetened almond butter

1½   tsp. pure vanilla extract

1. Preheat oven to 350°F. Spread almonds, oats, and rice cereal on baking sheet. Bake for 15 minutes, until toasted.

2. In large bowl, combine apricots, currants, and cinnamon. Toss to mix. Add toasted nuts, oats, and cereal and mix again.

3. Combine brown rice syrup and maple syrup in a saucepan. Bring to a boil over medium heat. Reduce heat to low and stir in almond butter and vanilla. Quickly pour syrup over oatmeal mixture and stir well.

4. With a spatula, spread the warm mixture over a baking sheet lined with parchment paper. Press into a thin, even layer. Place another piece of parchment on top. Work quickly because once the mixture cools, it will be hard to shape. Chill for 4 hours, then cut into squares. Bars can be refrigerated or frozen for up to 3 weeks.

< Homemade Energy Bars (at right in photo) and Everybody's Favorite Maple Bars (at left in photo; see recipe on p. 87)

Scrambled Eggs, Indian Style

My mother-in-law makes this for us when she comes to visit from India. We call these Dadi's ('dadi' means 'father's mother') Eggs, and they are great on whole wheat toast.

Serves 6

2	Tbsp. ghee (can be found at a specialty grocery store) or unsalted butter
1	onion, diced into ¼-in. pieces
1	tomato, diced into ¼-in. pieces
1	green chile, such as serrano, finely chopped
4	Tbsp. chopped cilantro, plus extra for garnish
1	tsp. sea salt
½	tsp. freshly ground black pepper
8	large eggs, whisked

1. Heat ghee in a large sauté pan. Sauté onion over low heat until translucent, about 5 minutes.

2. Add tomato and sauté until liquid has evaporated, about 4 minutes.

3. Add chiles and cilantro, then salt and pepper.

4. Add eggs and stir rapidly in circular motion until eggs are scrambled.

5. Garnish with cilantro and serve.

Barley and Maple Waffles

As with many batters, it is best to prepare this the night before to allow it to develop deeper flavor. I find that it also makes feeding hungry kids a lot easier. These are delicious served with Winter Fruit Compote (see recipe on p. 85), Rhubarb and Strawberry Compote (see recipe on p. 82), or Broiled Fruit, such as bananas (see recipe on p. 250).

Serves 6-8

2¼	cups whole-grain barley flour
¼	cup maple sugar
1	Tbsp. aluminum-free baking powder
1	tsp. sea salt
4	egg yolks from large eggs
1½	cups almond milk (or whole milk)
½	cup unsalted butter, melted
4	egg whites from large eggs

1. Sift together flour, sugar, baking powder, and salt into a large bowl.

2. In a medium bowl, beat egg yolks, milk, and melted butter.

3. Make a well in the center of the dry ingredients and add milk mixture.

4. Mix until just combined. Refrigerate for one hour or overnight.

5. In a medium bowl, whip the egg whites to soft peaks, for 4-5 minutes, and fold into batter.

6. Ladle batter onto a heated and greased waffle iron and cook until brown, about 5 minutes, then serve.

Soothing Chicken Congee

I discovered congee, a rice porridge usually served with chicken, scallions, and boiled peanuts, after taking a course on cooking to reduce inflammation. In Asia, breakfast foods are often very similar to lunch and dinner foods, so it is not unusual to see soups and stews or sushi served for breakfast. Congee is very healing. In Chinese cuisine, congee has long been used to cure upset stomachs and colds, and as a general tonic.

Serves 6

1   cup short-grain brown rice or Arborio rice, rinsed

6   cups water or chicken stock

8   oz. chicken, diced into ½-in. pieces (white or dark meat is fine; cooked chicken also works)

½   cup thinly sliced scallions, white and tender green parts

2   Tbsp. toasted sesame oil

1. Bring rice and water to a boil, lower heat, cover, and simmer for 1 hour, stirring frequently. You can do this the night before so that the next morning, you just need to add the chicken and some water.

2. Add chicken pieces and stir until cooked through, about 10 minutes.

3. Garnish with scallions and drizzle with toasted sesame oil.

 You can also make congee with other proteins such as firm-fleshed fish, or poached fruit such as pears or apples.

Vegetable Frittata

I like to use asparagus and mushrooms because I love the combination, but you can use any vegetables you like (onions and red peppers, spinach and bacon, red peppers and corn, etc.).

Serves 6

2	Tbsp. unsalted butter
1	onion, diced into ¼-in. pieces
1	cup button mushrooms, cut into ¼-in. slices
1½	cups asparagus, trimmed and cut into ½-in. lengths
8	large eggs
1	tsp. sea salt
½	tsp. freshly ground black pepper
½	cup Gruyère, grated
1	cup parmesan, grated
	Multi-grain crackers or whole-grain toast

1. Preheat broiler to 400°F.

2. Melt butter in a sauté pan. Add onion and sauté over low heat until soft and translucent, about 5 minutes.

3. Add mushrooms and sauté until soft, about 3 minutes. Add asparagus and continue to sauté until asparagus are soft, 3-6 minutes, depending on thickness.

4. Meanwhile, combine eggs, salt, pepper, Gruyère, and parmesan in a large bowl.

5. Add egg mixture to pan and cook until almost set, lifting edges of eggs so that liquid runs off the top and cooks.

6. Put pan in broiler and cook until frittata is puffed up and golden brown, 7-10 minutes.

7. Serve with multi-grain crackers or whole-grain toast.

Appetizers and Soups

I FIND IT REALLY INTERESTING that many cultures have some sort of food wrapped in dough: Greeks have spanakopita — spinach and cheese wrapped in phyllo dough; Italians have calzones—meat and tomatoes wrapped in dough; Indians have samosas—peas and potatoes wrapped in flaky wheat dough; Argentinians have empanadas—meat and vegetables wrapped in flaky wheat dough; Asians have spring rolls and dumplings; Jewish people have knishes; and Mexicans have burritos. The combinations are endless. I think there is something very warming and comforting about eating these foods. Maybe it's the idea of having a food wrapped in a warm blanket of dough. Another thing that is common to many cuisines throughout the world are bean dips. This is most likely because they are full of protein and can easily be eaten at any time of day.

Caramelized Onion and Gorgonzola Quiche

I like to serve quiche for brunch with a side salad. This filling—with the sweetness of the caramelized onions and the saltiness of the cheese—is a nice contrast of flavors.

Serves 6

1¼   cups whole-wheat pastry flour (or half whole-wheat and half all-purpose)

¼   tsp. sea salt

1/8   tsp. aluminum-free baking powder

8   Tbsp. unsalted butter, chilled and cut into small pieces

¼   cup ice water

2-3   Tbsp. Dijon mustard

Pastry Crust

1. In a large bowl, combine flour, salt, and baking powder and mix well.

2. Add butter and cut into flour with your fingertips until the mixture is crumbly.

3. Gradually add water and mix in slowly until the mixture comes together.

4. Gather the dough into a ball. Flatten into a round, wrap in plastic, and refrigerate for at least 1 hour.

5. Preheat oven to 350°F.

6. Roll the dough out on a well-floured counter and then place it a 10-in. tart pan. Don't worry if it breaks slightly, you can wet your hands and patch it together.

7. Pierce the dough all over with a fork and put a sheet of parchment on top of dough. Put pie weights or dried beans on top so that dough will not rise. Parbake dough until the sides of the crust start to brown, 20-25 minutes.

8. Remove beans and parchment and paint the bottom of the crust with mustard and bake for an additional 10-15 minutes.

3   Tbsp. unsalted butter

1-2 large onions, thinly sliced

½   cup Gorgonzola cheese,
     crumbled (optional)

4   large eggs, beaten

1   cup heavy cream

1   tsp. sea salt

½   tsp. freshly ground black
     pepper

½   cup Gruyère cheese,
     grated

Quiche Filling

1. Preheat oven to 350°F.

2. Melt butter in a large sauté pan. Add onion and cook over low heat until soft and slightly caramelized, about 20 minutes.

3. Spread onions over parbaked quiche crust. Sprinkle Gorgonzola on top (if using).

4. In a medium bowl, whisk eggs, cream, salt, and pepper. Pour over onions and Gorgonzola.

5. Sprinkle with Gruyère cheese.

6. Bake quiche 30-35 minutes until top is browned and knife inserted in center comes out clean.

7. Let cool for 5-10 minutes before serving.

You can fill the quiche with many other things, such as ham and cheese; or broccoli (blanched for 5 minutes in boiling, salted water to soften) and Cheddar instead of Gruyère cheese; or asparagus and Gruyère.

Indian Potato Samosas

Samosas are a family favorite. These can take some time to make, but the good thing is that they can be filled and frozen before being fried.

1½	cups organic unbleached all-purpose flour
½	tsp. sea salt
¼	tsp. aluminum-free baking powder
½	tsp. ajwain seeds (if you can't find this, you can use dried thyme)
4	Tbsp. unsalted butter
½	cup regular buttermilk (or 3 parts organic unhomogenized milk and 1 part yogurt)
	Samosa Filling
	Grapeseed oil

Samosa Dough

1. Mix flour, salt, baking powder, and ajwain in a large bowl. Add butter and cut into mixture with your fingertips until mixture is crumbly. Stir in just enough buttermilk to bring dough together, about ½ cup. Set aside in refrigerator for 1 hour. Meanwhile, make Samosa Filling.

2. Divide dough in half, roll each piece into a log, and cut each log into 7-8 pieces. Cover the cut pieces with a wet cloth or paper towel to prevent drying out.

3. Roll each piece into a 7-in. circle. Cut circle in half to make 2 semi-circles.

4. Moisten half of the straight edge of one semi-circle with a pastry brush dipped in water. Put 1 tsp. of filling in the middle of the semi-circle. Fold the other half over to form a cone. Press the dough together with your fingers to secure. Repeat with the rest of the pieces.

5. Set samosas on parchment-lined sheet pan and keep covered with damp cloth or plastic wrap.

6. Add ½ in. grapeseed oil to a large pan. Heat oil until it shimmers. Fry samosas 6-8 minutes on each side until golden-brown. The inside should be fully heated.

7. Remove with a slotted spoon, and put in a warm oven until ready to serve.

Samosa Filling

1. Melt ghee in a large sauté pan. Add mustard and cumin seeds. Cook until seeds start to pop, about 1 minute.

2. Add turmeric and cook for a few seconds.

3. Add jalapeño and onion and cook until soft. Add potatoes and stir to mix well. It is okay if the potatoes get mashed during cooking. Add garam masala and salt to taste. Add peas and cilantro and mix. Cool before filling the pastry.

Fills 30 samosas

2	Tbsp. ghee
1	tsp. black mustard seeds
½	tsp. cumin seeds
⅛	tsp. turmeric
½	jalapeño chile, finely chopped
½	Tbsp. ¼-in.-diced yellow onion
¾	lb. potatoes, cut into 1-in. cubes and boiled
½	tsp. garam masala (can be found any specialty grocery store)
1	tsp. sea salt
1	Tbsp. frozen peas
1½	Tbsp. minced fresh cilantro

Empanadas

Empanadas are delicious and so versatile. They can be served for meals but also make great lunchbox options, especially when accompanied by guacamole. Normally, they are served with a meat filling; however, you can also make a vegetarian filling with black beans.

Makes 12 pastries

2¼   cups organic, unbleached all-purpose flour

1½   tsp. sea salt

8   Tbsp. chilled, unsalted butter, cut into small cubes

2   large eggs

1/3   cup ice water

1   Tbsp. vinegar

Empanada meat filling or Empanada Black Bean and Corn Filling

1. Sift flour and salt into a large bowl. Rub butter in with your fingertips until mixture resembles coarse sand.

2. Beat together 1 of the eggs, water, and vinegar in a small bowl. Add to flour mixture and combine.

3. Turn mixture onto lightly floured surface and gather together, then knead gently with the heel of your hand. Form dough into a rectangle and chill at least 1 hour. Meanwhile, make filling (*see recipes on next page*).

4. Preheat oven to 400°F.

5. On a lightly floured surface, roll out the dough to ⅛ in. thick and cut out 4-in.-diameter rounds. Place 1½ Tbsp. filling on each round.

6. Beat the remaining egg and brush half of dough edge with it. Fold dough over filling to create a half-circle and seal edges with a fork.

7. Set empanadas on a baking sheet. Lightly brush with remaining egg.

8. Bake empanadas until golden, 25-30 minutes. Cool on wire rack and serve.

1	red onion, finely chopped
1	lb. ground beef or turkey
1	tomato, chopped
1	clove garlic, chopped
¼	tsp. cayenne pepper (optional)
½	tsp. chili pepper
½	tsp. ground cumin
½	tsp. dried oregano
1	tsp. sea salt
½	tsp. freshly ground black pepper
½	cup coarsely grated Monterey Jack cheese

Empanada Meat Filling

1. Sauté onion in a large skillet over medium heat until translucent, about 5 minutes. Add meat and sauté until cooked through and brown, breaking up meat with a fork.

2. Add tomato, garlic, and spices. Simmer until mixture is almost dry, 8-10 minutes, stirring occasionally. Season with salt and pepper. Cool completely and mix in cheese.

1	cup black beans, soaked overnight and drained
1½	Tbsp. cold-pressed extra-virgin olive oil
½	red onion, chopped
1	clove garlic, chopped
½	tsp. ground cumin
½	tomato, seeded and chopped
3	scallions, thinly sliced
1	ear of corn, kernels removed (or ½ cup frozen)
¼	cup Thompson raisins, soaked in warm water for 10 minutes
	Juice of ½ lime
4	oz. Monterey Jack cheese, grated
¼	cup chopped fresh cilantro

Empanada Black Bean and Corn Filling

1. Put the beans in a medium pot with cold water to cover. Bring to a boil, reduce heat, and cook beans until tender, 45 minutes to 1 hour. Drain.

2. Heat the olive oil in a large sauté pan, add onion, garlic, and cumin and sauté until very soft, about 5 minutes.

3. Add tomato and scallions and sauté an additional 5 minutes, until liquid has cooked away.

4. Add black beans, corn, raisins, and lime juice. Cook for another 5-7 minutes.

5. Remove from heat and let cool to room temperature in a cold water bath.

6. Stir in cheese and cilantro.

Spiced Chicken Quesadillas

This is a great way to use the chicken from Basic Chicken Stock (see recipe on p. 116). This is also a good lunchbox filler, or super-easy lunch option.

Serves 6

2	Tbsp. extra-virgin olive oil
1	red onion, finely sliced
1	red bell pepper, finely sliced
1	green chile, chopped (optional)
1	tsp. chili powder
¾	cup chopped fresh cilantro
1	tsp. sea salt
	Freshly ground black pepper to taste
1	cooked chicken, meat shredded
2	Tbsp. unsalted butter
6	whole-wheat or spelt tortillas
2	cups shredded Monterey Jack or Cheddar cheese
1	cup sour cream
	Juice of 1 lime

1. Heat olive oil in a sauté pan over medium heat. Sauté onion until soft, about 5 minutes.

2. Add red pepper and green chile and sauté until soft, about 4 minutes. Add chili powder, ¼ cup of the cilantro, salt and pepper.

3. Add chicken and cook until heated through. Stir to combine.

4. Preheat oven to 200°F.

5. Heat a large sauté pan over medium-low heat. Melt ½ tsp. of the butter in pan. Add 1-2 tortillas (depending on size of the pan). Place some of chicken mixture on half of the tortillas. Sprinkle some cheese on top. Close tortillas and flip to the other side. Cook until tortillas are lightly browned and cheese is starting to melt. Transfer the tortillas to a baking sheet and place sheet in the oven.

6. Repeat with remaining tortillas.

7. In a small bowl, mix the sour cream with the remaining cilantro and the lime juice.

8. Serve quesadillas with sour cream mixture on the side.

Vietnamese Fresh Spring Rolls

There are two main kinds of spring rolls in Vietnam: the fried ones and the fresh ones. Fried spring rolls are usually made with ground pork or shrimp with vegetables and then fried. Fresh spring rolls are made with lettuce, mint, bean sprouts, and shrimp, and are surprisingly full of flavor!

Makes 12 rolls

12	small or medium shrimp, peeled, deveined, and steamed
3½	oz. dried rice vermicelli noodles
12	sheets rice paper, 6 in. in diameter
12	Boston lettuce leaves, core removed, rinsed, and spun dry
12	fresh mint leaves, stemmed (if only small mint leaves are available, use 24)
8	oz. mung bean sprouts
	Nuoc Cham Nem Sauce (see recipe on p. 109)

1. Cut shrimp in half lengthwise.

2. Prepare dried noodles according to package directions and cut into small pieces.

3. Soften a sheet of rice paper by dipping into a pan of water and then draining on a flat, damp cloth. (Leave the sheets in the water for only a few seconds, because if you leave them too long, they will tear.)

4. Lay a lettuce leaf horizontally in the middle of the rice paper about 1 in. from the bottom of the sheet (the side closest to you), add 1 mint leaf (or 2 small leaves), 1 Tbsp. bean sprouts, and 1 Tbsp. rice noodles.

5. Fold left side of the rice paper into the middle, followed by the right side and bottom. Place half a shrimp on top.

6. Roll rice paper sheet up and over filling, and close wrapper. You may need some water to moisten rice paper.

7. Serve with Nuoc Cham Nem Sauce.

For the Nuoc Cham Nem Sauce

2	cloves garlic, chopped
½	fresh red chile pepper, seeded and finely chopped
¼	cup fish sauce
¹/₈	cup rice vinegar
¹/₃	cup water
1½	Tbsp. palm sugar (available at specialty food stores, or use Sucanat)
½	carrot, grated
¼	cup green unripe papaya or daikon radish, grated
¼	tsp. freshly ground black pepper

Nuoc Cham Nem Sauce

1. Combine garlic, chile pepper, fish sauce, vinegar, water, sugar, carrot, papaya (or radish), and pepper in a bowl and mix well.

2. Put sauce in a bowl for dipping.

Savory Buckwheat Ham and Cheese Crêpes

Crêpes make a great appetizer and are also good served with a salad for a light meal or as a dessert. Crêpes can be eaten dusted with maple sugar, jam, or honey or filled with ham and cheese. Another option for a more substantial meal is to fill them with ham and cheese and cover them with Béchamel (see recipe on p. 191), then bake for 20 minutes.

Makes fifteen 6-in. crêpes

3	large eggs
1¼	cup whole milk
¾	cup buckwheat flour
¼	cup organic, unbleached all-purpose flour (if you want to make these gluten-free, you can use millet flour)
½	tsp. sea salt
4	Tbsp. melted unsalted butter
2	cups ham, diced
2	cups grated Gruyère cheese

1. In a medium bowl, combine eggs and milk and whisk until blended.

2. In a large bowl, combine flour and salt. Make a well in the center of the dry ingredients, then add milk and egg mixture slowly, whisking constantly.

3. Refrigerate for 30 minutes.

4. Remove from refrigerator and stir in 2 Tbsp. of the melted butter.

5. Pour ½ tsp. melted butter into crêpe pan or small frying pan, swirl around to coat entire pan. (Use a little more butter if necessary.)

6. Add 2-3 Tbsp. of batter to the pan, depending on the size of the pan (you only want to coat the pan thinly). Quickly swirl the batter to form a thin, round pancake. Cook 2-3 minutes. Turn crêpe and continue to cook another 2-3 minutes until

I prefer to use buckwheat flour because it is a whole-grain flour. Buckwheat is actually not related to wheat, so it's a good gluten-free option for those who are allergic or sensitive to gluten.

done. If you are filling the crêpe with ham and cheese, add the filling when you turn the crêpe.

7. Repeat with remaining batter.

8. If serving for dessert, omit the ham and cheese and dust with confectioners' sugar or spread with jam or honey and serve.

Curried Chicken Salad

This is another good way to use the chicken from the Basic Chicken Stock (see recipe on p. 116), and also a tasty lunchbox filler.

Serves 6

2	cups cooked, shredded chicken
½	cup expeller-pressed mayonnaise
½	cup plain, full-fat yogurt
1	Tbsp. fresh lime juice
5	tsp. curry powder
1	shallot, finely chopped
½	cup grapes, halved
2	celery stalks, diced into ¼-in. cubes
	Cilantro, for garnish

1. Combine chicken, mayonnaise, yogurt, lime juice, curry powder, shallot, grapes, and celery in a bowl and mix well.

2. Garnish with cilantro and serve.

Classic Guacamole

My youngest daughter, who is six, loves to "make" this guacamole. I prepare all the ingredients for her and she mixes everything together. It is very easy to make and goes well with empanadas, quesadillas, and chili.

Makes about 2 cups

3   medium Haas avocados, peeled and mashed with a potato masher

2   tomatoes, diced

1   onion, finely chopped

1   jalapeño chile, finely chopped

1   clove garlic, smashed and minced

Juice of 1 lime (about 2 Tbsp.)

2   tsp. extra-virgin olive oil

2   Tbsp. chopped fresh cilantro, plus leaves for garnish

1   tsp. sea salt

Freshly ground back pepper to taste

1. Combine avocados, tomatoes, onion, chile, garlic, lime juice, olive oil, cilantro salt, and pepper in a medium bowl and mix well.

2. Garnish with cilantro leaves and serve with tortilla chips, empanadas, or chicken quesadillas.

Provençal Olive Tapenade

This is a classic French recipe that goes well with crackers or grissini breadsticks.

Makes about 1 cup

2	cups pitted Niçoise olives in olive oil
2	Tbsp. capers
2	anchovies (optional, a good source of Omega-3 fatty acids)
1	clove garlic
2	Tbsp. extra-virgin olive oil
1	Tbsp. fresh lemon juice
	Freshly ground black pepper to taste

1. Combine olives, capers, anchovies (if using), garlic, olive oil, lemon juice, and pepper in a blender and blend to a smooth paste.

2. Serve with grissini breadsticks or crudités.

White Bean Dip

This is a good alternative to hummus and also very easy to make.

Makes about 2 cups

1	cup dried white beans (cannellini or navy), soaked overnight
1	medium onion
1	clove garlic
	Juice of 1 lemon (about 4 Tbsp.)
¼	cup extra-virgin olive oil
1	tsp. sea salt
¼	cup chopped chives

1. Put the beans in a medium pot with cold water to cover. Bring to a boil, reduce heat, and cook beans until tender, 45 minutes to 1 hour.

2. Combine beans, onion, garlic, lemon juice, olive oil, and salt in a blender and blend until creamy.

3. Add chives and mix well.

4. Serve with crudités or grissini bread sticks.

Traditional Hummus

A classic recipe and super-easy to make, this is my favorite dip and one of my children's preferred lunchbox options.

Makes about 2 cups

1	cup dried chickpeas, soaked overnight
1	cup extra-virgin olive oil, plus more for garnish
1/3	cup tahini
1	clove garlic
	Juice of 1 lemon (about 4 Tbsp.)
1	tsp. ground cumin
1	tsp. sea salt
	Freshly ground black pepper to taste
	Paprika, for garnish

1. Put the chickpeas in a medium pot with cold water to cover. Bring to a boil, reduce heat, and cook beans until tender, 45 minutes to 1 hour. Drain, reserving some of the cooking water.

2. Combine chickpeas, olive oil, tahini, garlic, lemon juice, cumin, salt, and pepper in a blender and blend to a smooth paste. If you need more liquid, you can use more olive oil or some of the chickpea cooking water.

3. Garnish with a drizzle of olive oil and a sprinkle of paprika, and serve with your favorite crudités.

Basic Chicken Stock

This is an essential item for your kitchen because you can use it for so many things, from soups to sauces and rice dishes. I usually make a pot of chicken stock every other week and freeze it so that I have some whenever needed. You can follow the same process for vegetable stock, omitting the chicken.

Makes 12-16 cups

1	whole chicken
2	leeks, roughly sliced
2	carrots, roughly sliced
2	celery ribs, roughly sliced
1	fennel bulb, quartered
1	onion, halved
1	bouquet garni (2 bay leaves, 10 black peppercorns, 6 parsley stems, 2 thyme sprigs wrapped in a leek leaf or in cheesecloth)

1. Combine all ingredients in a large pot. Add cold water to cover.

2. Bring to a boil and simmer 1 hour, skimming froth at the surface when necessary and turning chicken occasionally to ensure that it is fully cooked.

3. Pour stock through a fine-mesh sieve into containers and discard solids.

 I prefer to eat free-range chicken that is certified organic. This means that the bird has not consumed any antibiotics or genetically-modified feed, nor been exposed to pesticides or inhumane conditions. If you can't find certified organic poultry, then at least make sure that the chicken is antibiotic- and chemical-free.

Warming and Healing Chicken Soup

Chicken soup is my first remedy for a cold (and pretty much any other ailment!) because according to Hanna Kroeger, a pioneer in holistic healing, "chicken soup has a natural ingredient which feeds, repairs and calms the mucouse [sic] lining in the small intestine... [sic]. Chicken soup...heals the nerves, improves digestion, reduces allergies, relaxes, and gives strength."[34] Moreover, according to nutritionist Johnny Bowden, research has shown that the ingredients in chicken soup stop the movement of white blood cells, called neutrophils, that are released when you have an infection or a cold, reducing many cold symptoms.[35] Besides all the scientific stuff, chicken soup just tastes good.

Serves 6

2	onions, finely chopped
2	Tbsp. extra-virgin olive oil or unsalted butter
2	carrots, peeled and finely chopped
2	celery stalks, finely chopped
	Parsnips, potatoes, turnips, or other root vegetables (optional)
2-3	chicken breasts or boned chicken thighs, cut into bite-size pieces
2	Tbsp. chopped fresh parsley
2	sprigs fresh thyme
4-6	cups chicken stock
	Cooked noodles or rice (optional)
1	tsp. sea salt
	Freshly ground black pepper to taste

1. In a large pot, sauté onions in olive oil or butter until golden, about 5 minutes. Add carrots and celery and sauté until they have some color, about 4 minutes.

2. Add parsnips, potatoes, turnips, or other root vegetables (if using) and sauté for 5-6 minutes.

3. Add chicken pieces, parsley, and thyme sprigs and cover with chicken stock or a combination of stock and water.

4. Bring to a boil, lower heat, and simmer, covered, until chicken is fully cooked, 15-20 minutes. If you want, you can also add some cooked noodles or rice at this point.

5. Season with salt and pepper.

French Soupe au Pistou

This is a traditional French vegetable and bean soup. There are many variations of this soup in other Mediterranean cuisines. It is light and refreshing yet substantial enough to be a meal in itself.

Serves 6-8

1	cup dried white beans such as cannellini or navy beans, soaked overnight and drained
2	medium yellow onions, 1 halved and 1 chopped
4	cloves garlic, 2 chopped and 2 minced
1	dried bay leaf
11	cups water
4	Tbsp. extra-virgin olive oil
1	fennel bulb, core and ends removed, cut into ½-in. cubes
2	red potatoes, cut into ½-in. cubes
4	small zucchini, cut into ½-in. cubes
¾	lb. green beans, cut into ½-in. pieces
3	vine tomatoes, cut into ¼-in. cubes
1	tsp. sea salt
	Freshly ground pepper to taste
1	cup Pistou (see recipe on p. 120)

1. Put white beans, halved whole onion, chopped garlic, and bay leaf in a medium saucepan. Add 3 cups of the water and bring to a boil over high heat. Reduce heat to low, cover the saucepan, and simmer until the beans are tender, 1-1½ hours. Discard onion, garlic, and bay leaf. Drain beans and reserve the liquid.

2. Meanwhile, in a large, heavy pot, heat olive oil over medium heat. Add fennel, potatoes, chopped onion, and minced garlic. Sauté vegetables over low heat until they are softened, about 10 minutes. Add remaining water and gradually bring to a boil. Reduce the heat and simmer for 30 minutes.

3. Add zucchini and green beans to the pot and simmer for 10 minutes. Mash the potatoes against the side of the pot using a large fork (the potatoes will thicken the soup). Add the diced tomatoes and the white beans with their cooking liquid and simmer the soup over moderately low heat for 5-10 minutes. Season with salt and pepper.

4. Add pistou to soup and serve.

Pistou

1   Tbsp. minced garlic

1   tsp. sea salt

4½   cups fresh basil leaves, torn into small pieces

¼   cup grated tomatoes

¼   cup extra-virgin olive oil

1   cup Mimolette cheese or aged Gouda, grated

1. In a large mortar, pound the garlic with the salt to a paste. Add handfuls of basil and mash against the side of the mortar until almost smooth.

2. Stir in tomatoes, then gradually stir in olive oil until it is incorporated. Stir in cheese and refrigerate until ready to serve.

 You can also do this in a food processor or blender, but the texture is not as nice.

Summer Fresh Pesto

Pistou is very similar to pesto sauce. In summer, when basil is abundant, I love to make a pesto to add to pasta, vegetables, or soups. You can also use it as a sauce for poached fish or chicken.

Makes 1 cup

2   oz. fresh basil (or arugula)

2   cloves garlic

2   Tbsp. pine nuts or walnuts

1   tsp. sea salt

½   cup extra-virgin olive oil

2   Tbsp. freshly grated parmesan

1. Put basil, garlic, pine nuts or walnuts, salt, and olive oil in the blender and blend to a smooth paste.

2. Mix in parmesan.

Vichyssoise

This classic soup is a family favorite. I don't make it often because it's so rich, but when I do, it's gone in an instant. Traditional Vichyssoise has a lot of cream; however, the soup is just as good without it.

Serves 6

2	Tbsp. unsalted butter
1	medium onion, coarsely sliced
1	lb. leeks, white and light-green parts only, roughly sliced
1	tsp. sea salt
	Freshly ground black pepper to taste
1	lb. potatoes, coarsely sliced and soaked in cold water until ready to use (this will prevent them from browning)
4	cups Basic Chicken Stock (see recipe on p. 116)
1½	cups unhomogenized organic milk
½-¾	cups heavy cream (optional)
	Medium bunch of chives, sliced

1. Melt butter in a large pot and add the onions, leeks, salt, and pepper and cook, stirring occasionally, until soft but not brown, 7-10 minutes.

2. Drain potato slices in a colander and then immediately transfer them to the pot.

3. Add stock, and bring to a boil. Cover and simmer, stirring occasionally, until the potatoes are very tender when pierced with the tip of the small knife, about 30 minutes.

4. Let soup cool a bit. Working in batches, purée until smooth in a blender or food processor. If the leek is very fibrous, you may want to strain the soup.

5. Return soup to the pot, add milk, and bring to barely a simmer. If it's very thick, you can add ½ - ¾ cup water or cream or a combination.

6. Season to taste with salt and pepper and chill thoroughly. Garnish with chives and serve.

It is best to get potatoes that are not too starchy, such as Yukon Gold, to prevent the soup from becoming gelatinous.

Carrot-Ginger Soup

This is another soup I find very comforting. The best thing is that you can easily substitute squash or sweet potatoes for the carrots, or add parsnips in addition to the carrots.

Serves 6

1½ Tbsp. extra-virgin olive oil

3-4 shallots, coarsely sliced

¾ cup leeks, white and light-green parts only, coarsely sliced

6 carrots, peeled and coarsely chopped (alternatively, use pumpkin or squash)

½ apple, peeled and diced (I prefer the tart Granny Smith variety)

4 cups vegetable or Basic Chicken Stock (see recipe on p. 116), or water

1 ½-in. piece fresh ginger, grated on a Microplane

2 Tbsp. fresh lemon juice

1 tsp. sea salt

Freshly ground black pepper to taste

Cilantro leaves for garnish (optional)

1. In a large saucepan, heat olive oil over medium-low heat. Add shallots and leeks. Cook, stirring occasionally, until vegetables are softened but not browned, about 5 minutes.

2. Stir in carrots and apple and cook over low heat until carrots are soft, 15-20 minutes.

3. Add stock or water. Bring to a simmer, uncovered, over medium-high heat. Reduce heat to low and simmer gently for 10 minutes. Add ginger.

4. Let soup cool a bit. Working in batches, purée until smooth in a blender or food processor. Pour each batch of puréed soup through a sieve into a bowl or pot. Use a rubber spatula to help the soup pass through.

5. Season with lemon juice, salt, and pepper. Garnish with cilantro leaves, if you like, and serve.

French Lentil Soup

On New Year's Day in France, it is customary to eat lentils to ensure prosperity for the upcoming year.

Serves 6

1	cup French du Puy lentils or small brown lentils
2	Tbsp. extra-virgin olive oil
2	onions, chopped into ¼-in. dice
2	cups leeks, white and light-green parts only, thinly sliced
2-3	cloves garlic, minced
1	tsp. sea salt
½	tsp. freshly ground black pepper
2	tsp. fresh thyme leaves or 1 tsp. dry
2	celery ribs, cut into ¼-in. dice
2	carrots, peeled and cut into ¼-in. dice
4	cups water, vegetable stock or Basic Chicken Stock (see recipe on p. 116)
2	Tbsp. tomato paste
2-3	all-beef, nitrite- and nitrate-free frankfurters (optional), cut into 1-in. pieces
1	Tbsp. sherry vinegar
	Grated parmesan

1. In a large bowl, cover lentils with boiling water and allow to sit for 15 minutes. Drain.

2. Heat olive oil in a large pot and sauté the onions, leeks, garlic, salt, pepper, and thyme until vegetables are soft but not browned, about 10 minutes.

3. Add celery and carrots and sauté for another 10 minutes. Add water or stock, tomato paste, and lentils. Cover and bring to a boil. Reduce heat and simmer uncovered for 1 hour, or until lentils are cooked through and tender. Add the frankfurters (if using) and heat through.

4. Add sherry vinegar. Sprinkle with grated parmesan just before serving.

Easy Vegetable Soups

You can make some simple and delicious soups by sautéing onions, shallots, or leeks, then adding a vegetable of choice and enough chicken or vegetable stock to cover. Bring to a boil, lower heat, and simmer until vegetables are soft. For a thicker soup, you can add a peeled and cubed potato. Let cool and blend until smooth. If you want, add some herbs to the soup. In summer, you can chill the soup. The following recipes provide some simple variations.

Chilled Zucchini Soup

This is a light soup that is very refreshing in summer.

Serves 6

¼	cup extra-virgin olive oil
1-2	shallots, coarsely chopped
2	lb. zucchini, roughly chopped
	Zest of 2 lemons, about 3 Tbsp.
4	cups vegetable or Basic Chicken Stock (see recipe on p. 116)
1	cup fresh parsley or fresh cilantro, roughly chopped
1	tsp. sea salt
	Freshly ground black pepper to taste
½	cup crème fraîche or sour cream (optional)

1. Heat olive oil in a large pot. Add shallots and sauté until soft.

2. Add zucchini and lemon zest. Sauté for 2 minutes.

3. Add stock to cover and bring to a boil. Lower heat, cover, and simmer until zucchini is soft, about 10 minutes.

4. Add parsley or cilantro and remove soup from heat. Let cool.

5. Place cooled soup in blender and blend until smooth. Add salt, pepper, and crème fraîche (if using).

6. Refrigerate until cool and serve.

Chilled Pea Soup

This soup can be also served hot.

Serves 6

2	Tbsp. unsalted butter
2	medium onions, thinly sliced
3	cups frozen peas
4	cups vegetable or Basic Chicken Stock (see recipe on p. 116)
¼	cup fresh tarragon or mint, chopped
1	tsp. sea salt
	Freshly ground black pepper to taste

1. Melt butter in a large pan over medium heat, then add onions. Sauté until soft, about 6 minutes.

2. Add peas and sauté 1 minute.

3. Add stock and bring to a boil. Lower heat, cover, and simmer until peas are cooked, about 10 minutes.

4. Add tarragon or mint, salt, and pepper. Let cool.

5. Pour cooled soup in blender and blend until smooth.

6. Refrigerate until cold, then serve.

Cooling Gazpacho Soup

This soup is very refreshing in summer. The bread gives it a nice texture and makes it quite filling. A simple green salad is a delicious accompaniment.

Serves 6

3	lb. vine tomatoes, peeled and roughly chopped
1	clove garlic
½	red onion, quartered
1	green pepper, half seeded and halved and the other half seeded and cut into ¼-in. dice
1	cucumber, half seeded and cut into large chunks and the other half seeded and cut into ¼-in. dice
1	cup extra-virgin olive oil
1½	Tbsp. balsamic vinegar
2	slices whole-wheat bread (preferably a bit stale)
½	cup cold water
½	tsp. ground roasted cumin
1	tsp. sea salt
	Freshly ground black pepper to taste

1. Put tomatoes, garlic, onion, large pieces of green pepper, cucumber chunks, olive oil, and vinegar in a blender and blend to purée.

2. Tear bread into small chunks and soak in cold water. Squeeze out water and add to blender, along with cumin. Pulse a few more times until soup is smooth.

3. Season with salt and pepper, and garnish with diced green pepper and cucumber.

Mexican Shrimp Cocktail

This is somewhere between a soup and an appetizer. I love to make this for summer parties because it's so refreshing.

Serves 6

1	quart 100% tomato juice
¼	cup tomato paste
4-5	scallions, white parts only, thinly sliced
½	red onion, cut into ¼-in. dice
1	cucumber, seeded and cut into ¼-in. dice
1	medium avocado, peeled and cut into ¼-in. dice
1	lb. small or medium shrimp, peeled, deveined and cooked
4	Tbsp. chopped fresh cilantro

1. Combine ingredients in a large bowl and mix well.

2. Serve in martini glasses with organic tortilla chips.

Southwestern Black Bean Soup

This is a very hearty soup that goes well with Cornbread (see recipe on p. 150). It is particularly nice on a winter's day.

Serves 6

2   cups black beans, soaked overnight and drained

½   cup diced bacon

1   large onion, chopped

2   cloves garlic, minced

2   jalapeño peppers, finely chopped

4   cups vegetable stock or Basic Chicken Stock (see recipe on p. 116)

½   cup Jerez sherry

¼   cup chopped fresh cilantro

1. Put the beans in a medium pot with cold water to cover. Bring to a boil, reduce heat, and cook beans until tender, 45 minutes to 1 hour.

2. Cook bacon in a large pot over medium heat until just starting to brown. Remove bacon and leave the fat in the pan. Add onion, garlic, and jalapeño peppers to bacon fat, and cook until vegetables soften, about 10 minutes.

3. Add cooked beans, stock, and sherry to pot.

4. Bring soup to simmer and let cook 5 minutes. Add cilantro and serve.

Miso Soup

Made from fermented soy, rice, and/or barley, miso is high in protein, manganese, and vitamin K, which is essential for blood clotting and bone mineralization. Besides all that, miso is very nourishing.

Serves 6

Handful of wakame seaweed, about 3 oz.

2   medium carrots, peeled and sliced into thin rounds

1   head broccoli, cut into small florets, stems peeled and chopped

2   Tbsp. light miso paste

4   scallions, white and light-green parts only, thinly sliced

½   tsp. sea salt

Freshly ground black pepper to taste

1. Bring large pot of water to a boil.

2. Add wakame, carrots, and broccoli stems and simmer until soft, 2 minutes.

3. Add broccoli florets and simmer an additional 3-4 minutes, until broccoli is soft. The broccoli should still be bright green.

4. Add miso and scallions and turn off heat.

5. Season with salt and pepper and serve.

Miso and seaweed are quite salty so it is best to start with less salt and add more as necessary.

Comforting and Soothing Dal

Dal and rice are a complete protein source, so a bowl of dal and rice can easily be a meal. I have to confess that the first time I made dal, I refused to heed my husband's advice to add more water, insisting that I should follow the recipe. Well, my dal became as hard as a rock and it was about 10 years before I tried to make it again. Fortunately, my subsequent attempts were successful.

Serves 6

1½	cups red or yellow lentils
½	tsp. turmeric
4	cups water
1	medium tomato, chopped
1	tsp. sea salt
3	Tbsp. ghee
1	tsp. cumin seeds
1	onion, chopped
6	cloves garlic, thinly sliced
¼	tsp. cayenne pepper
1	tsp. garam masala
¼	cup chopped fresh cilantro

1. Combine lentils and turmeric in water and cook until soft, 25-30 minutes. Add additional water if liquid has evaporated and/or lentils are dry.

2. Add tomato and salt and cook an additional 5 minutes.

3. In a small pan, heat ghee over medium heat. When hot, add cumin seeds.

4. When cumin seeds start to pop, add onion and garlic. Sauté until soft, about 6 minutes.

5. Add cayenne and garam masala.

6. Add the mixture, called tarka, to lentils, then stir in cilantro.

7. Remove from heat and serve.

 In India, a mixture of fried onions, garlic, and spices is added to the dal at the very end. This mixture is called a tarka, and it is similar to the pistou added to French Soupe au Pistou (see recipe on p. 118). It serves to "lift" the flavors in the soup.

Black Dal

You can make dal using any type of lentil you want — red, yellow, green, or black. The traditional way of making this black dal uses a lot of cream, which I prefer to avoid. Instead, I add a little more ghee. This dal is very rich, so I make it only occasionally, but it is very flavorful and goes well with plain rice.

Serves 6

1	cup split black lentils, soaked overnight
3	cups water
¼	cup ghee
1	tsp. cumin seeds
1	onion, chopped
3	cloves garlic, minced
1	1-in. piece of fresh ginger, grated on a Microplane
1	medium tomato, diced
1	tsp. garam masala
1	tsp. sea salt

1. Cook lentils in a large pot of water until soft, 30-45 minutes. Purée half of the lentils and return to pot.

2. Heat ghee in a sauté pan over medium heat. Add cumin seeds and let sizzle for about 1 minute.

3. Add onion, garlic, and ginger. Sauté on medium heat until soft, about 5 minutes.

4. Add tomato, garam masala, and salt, then sauté an additional 2-3 minutes.

5. Add this mixture to the pot with lentils, mix well, and serve.

Asian Vegetable Soup

Like miso, this soup is very light and refreshing, as well as nourishing.

Serves 6

6	cups vegetable or Basic Chicken Stock (see recipe on p. 116), or water
1	1-in. piece of fresh ginger, grated on a Microplane
1	Tbsp. thinly sliced lemon-grass
2	carrots, cut on the diagonal into ¼-in. slices
1	head broccoli
1	cup button mushrooms, halved
½	head green cabbage, shredded
½	lb. firm tofu, cut into ½-in. cubes
½	cup chopped fresh cilantro
½	cup scallions, white and light-green parts only, thinly sliced
4	Tbsp. tamari soy sauce

1. Combine stock or water, ginger, lemon-grass, and carrots in a large pot and set over medium heat.

2. Trim and peel the broccoli stalks. Cut the tops into small florets. Cut the thin stalks lengthwise in half and the thick ones into 4 spears. Cut stalks into ¼-in. slices and add to pot. When soup has come to a boil, add florets, mushrooms, cabbage, and tofu.

3. Simmer 10-15 minutes until vegetables are tender.

4. Stir in cilantro, scallions, and soy sauce. Serve.

Chickpea and Vegetable Tagine, p. 184

Entrées

I HAVE CHOSEN MY FAVORITE ENTRÉES for this section of the book. You'll find them organized by main dishes, grain and bean dishes, and vegetable dishes. They represent flavors and cuisines from many parts of the world and are strongly based on the traditional dishes from these varied cultures. They are delicious, healthy, and simple and will feed you and your family in deeply satisfying ways.

MEAT, POULTRY & FISH

THERE ARE SO MANY DISHES THAT I LOVE AND LOVE TO MAKE that it's hard to select just a few. I've tried to provide a sampling of varied, healthy dishes. Some take longer than others to make, and for those it's best to plan ahead. If I don't have much time, I simply broil a piece of grass-fed beef or lamb seasoned with whole-grain mustard, Worcestershire sauce, sea salt, and pepper, and serve it with steamed vegetables and salad.

Hearty Beef Stew

I love stews and curries because I find them comforting. They are easy to digest, so they are very nourishing when your immune system is compromised. It is best to start this recipe a day ahead because you want to marinate the beef in a red wine marinade to tenderize it and give it wonderful flavor.

Serves 6

For the marinade

2	carrots, sliced
1-2	celery ribs, sliced
½	onion, chopped
3	Tbsp. extra-virgin olive oil
2	Tbsp. mixed herbs (parsley, thyme, and bay leaf)
20	black peppercorns, about 2 tsp.
1-2	cloves garlic, chopped
2	cups red wine
1	tsp. sea salt

For the stew

2	lb. beef chuck, cut into cubes
4	cups crushed tomatoes
1	bouquet garni (bay leaf, parsley sprigs, and thyme wrapped in cheesecloth or in a leek leaf)
½	cup chopped bacon
2	onions, sliced
¼	lb. button mushrooms, sliced
1	tsp. sea salt
	Freshly ground black pepper to taste
2	Tbsp. chopped fresh parsley

Make the marinade

1. The day before, in a large pot, over low heat, sauté carrots, celery, and onion in olive oil. Add herbs, peppercorns, and garlic and cook, stirring, until they become fragrant. Add wine and salt and bring to a boil. Simmer for 10-15 minutes. Remove from heat and cool.

2. Place beef cubes in bowl and pour cooled marinade over them. Refrigerate overnight.

Make the stew

1. Preheat oven to 350°F.

2. Place meat and marinade in heavy casserole. Add tomatoes and bouquet garni. Cover. Set casserole in oven to cook. After 1 hour, lower temperature to 250°F and cook for 3-4 more hours.

CONTINUED >

3. In the meantime, sauté bacon in a large frying pan. When lightly browned add onion and sauté until soft, about 5 minutes. Add mushrooms, salt, and pepper and sauté an additional 3-5 minutes, until mushrooms are browned and have released their juices.

4. Set casserole on top of stove over low heat. Add bacon, onions, and mushrooms. Continue cooking for an additional 15 minutes. Remove bouquet garni and skim grease from the top of cooking liquid. Adjust seasoning. Sprinkle with chopped parsley and serve.

Asian Beef and Vegetable Stir-Fry

Quick-cooking methods are very common in China. They are meant to save scarce fuel and more important, to release all the vitamins and nutrients in a food. In this way, you get the benefits of almost raw foods, with their vitamins and nutrients intact, without the "cooling" effect of the foods.

Serves 6

1½	Tbsp. kuzu root starch (this can be found in Japanese or specialty food stores)
3	Tbsp. tamari soy sauce
1½	Tbsp. rice wine
1/3	tsp. maple sugar
1/3	tsp. sea salt
1/3	tsp. freshly ground black pepper
6	Tbsp. unrefined sesame oil
2	lb. flank steak, sliced into 2-in. strips along the grain
1	2-3 -in. piece of ginger, cut into julienne strips, 1-1½ in. long
4	cloves garlic, chopped
¼	lb. broccoli, cut into small florets
¼	lb. carrots, cut into julienne strips, 1-1½ in. long
1	red pepper, cut into thin strips
¼	lb. sugar snap peas, trimmed and cut into 1-in. lengths
3	Tbsp. scallions, cut into 1-in. lengths
2/3	cup Basic Chicken Stock (see recipe on p. 116)
2	Tbsp. sherry
	Toasted sesame oil for garnish

1. In a bowl, mix the kuzu root starch with the soy sauce, rice wine, sugar, salt, pepper, and 2 Tbsp. of the sesame oil. Add the beef and toss to coat.

2. Heat 2 Tbsp. of the sesame oil in a wok over high heat. Add the beef in one layer and cook undisturbed until it begins to brown, about 1 minute. Remove the beef and transfer to a bowl.

3. Add the remaining oil to the wok. Add the ginger and garlic and stir-fry until very fragrant, about 15 seconds. Add the broccoli, carrots, red pepper, snap peas, and scallions and sauté 2 minutes.

4. Add chicken stock and sherry, lower heat, and cover. Cook for 5-7 minutes, until vegetables are just done.

5. Return beef to wok and stir-fry until heated through.

6. Garnish with toasted sesame oil and serve.

Japanese Beef Curry

Asian curries and stews generally have more spices than Western ones. All the spices in the curries have healing properties that also help support digestion and the immune system. I serve this with Japanese short-grain brown rice.

Serves 6

2	Tbsp. extra-virgin olive oil
2	onions, sliced ⅛-in. thick
2	lb. boneless beef, chicken, or tofu, cut into 1-in. cubes
4	carrots, sliced diagonally into rounds
2	Yukon Gold potatoes, peeled and cut into ¾-in. cubes
4-5	cups Basic Chicken Stock (see recipe on p. 116) or water
1	apple, peeled, cored, and grated
2	tsp. sea salt
1	tsp. garam masala
¼	cup curry paste

For the curry paste

¼	cup unsalted butter
¼	cup organic unbleached all-purpose flour
2	Tbsp. curry powder
¼	tsp. cayenne
¼	tsp. black pepper
1	Tbsp. tomato paste
1	Tbsp. Worcestershire sauce or tonkatsu sauce

1. Heat olive oil in a large saucepan over medium heat. Add the onions and sauté until golden-brown, about 8 minutes.

2. Turn the heat to high and add the beef or chicken. Sauté until browned on all sides. If you are using tofu, add it after you have cooked the vegetables. Add the carrots, potatoes, and chicken stock or water and bring to a boil.

3. Add the grated apple, salt, and garam masala. Lower heat and simmer for 30 minutes or until carrots and potatoes are soft. Add more water if necessary.

Make the curry paste

4. Melt the butter in a small saucepan over medium heat. Add the flour and curry powder and stir until mixture forms a thick paste.

5. Add the cayenne, black pepper, tomato paste, and Worcestershire sauce. Continue to cook until mixture is crumbly, 3-4 minutes. Remove from heat.

7. Ladle some of the curry sauce into the curry paste and whisk until smooth.

4. Pour the mixture into pot with meat and vegetables and stir until thickened. Serve.

Thai Chicken in Green Curry Sauce

The native coconut has always been important in Southeast Asian cuisine. It contains lauric acid, a healthy fatty acid with antibacterial and anti-microbial properties. In warm climates, it was important to use ingredients with these properties to help prevent food poisoning.

Serves 6

6	boneless chicken breasts
3	13.5-oz. cans coconut milk
2	cups Thai Green Curry Paste (see recipe on p.146)
2	cups mixed vegetables, cut into small pieces, such as sliced carrots, snow peas, broccoli florets, or baby corn
3	Tbsp. fish sauce
3	Tbsp. palm sugar
6	wild lime leaves, sliced thin (these can usually be found in specialty stores)
1	tsp. sea salt
3	red bell peppers, sliced thin
¾	cup thinly sliced Thai or regular basil
1	Thai red chile, diced (optional)

1. Cut chicken into bite-size chunks.

2. Heat coconut milk in a large saucepan. Add Thai Green Curry Paste and cook for a minute, until well mixed. Add chicken pieces and cook 1-2 minutes to infuse chicken with flavor.

3. Add vegetables, fish sauce, palm sugar, lime leaves, and salt. Simmer until vegetables are tender and chicken is done, 8-10 minutes. Add red pepper and cook 1 minute longer.

4. Scatter basil into curry along with chile pepper, if using.

Thai Green Curry Paste

½	Tbsp. coriander seeds
½	tsp. cumin seeds
½	tsp. black peppercorns
1	lemongrass stalk, sliced thin
2	Tbsp. cilantro, stems only
1	½-in. piece fresh ginger, chopped
1	tsp. lime zest
½	Tbsp. fresh squeezed lime juice
5-6	cloves garlic, chopped
2	shallots, chopped
½	tsp. shrimp paste (can usually be found in specialty stores)
1	tsp. fish sauce
½	tsp. palm sugar

1. In blender, grind ingredients into paste, about 2 minutes.

 Many traditional Asian cuisines use spice mixes as the foundation for dishes. They infuse a lot of flavor into simple dishes and can be stored for up to 2 weeks in the refrigerator. Thai green curry paste can be used to make shrimp or chicken in a green curry sauce, or it can be used as a soup base or seasoning for stir-fries.

Chicken Curry with Fruit

This is a chicken curry recipe that my mom used to make. It's not a very traditional recipe because it includes fruit, but I really love the combination of salty and sweet.

Serves 6

1	onion, cut into ¼-in. dice
6	Tbsp. extra virgin olive oil
2	Tbsp. organic, un-bleached all-purpose flour
3-4	Tbsp. curry powder
1	Tbsp. white wine
½	cup Basic Chicken Stock (see recipe on p. 116)
1	apple, peeled, cored, and grated
1	cup plain, full-fat yogurt
1½	lb. chicken pieces (I prefer boneless thighs)
3-4	cups fruit, cut into 1-in. pieces (any combination; pineapples, mangos, apples, and pears are good choices)

1. In a large saucepan, sauté onion in 2 Tbsp. of the olive oil until translucent, about 5 minutes. Add flour and stir gently so it browns lightly.

2. Add curry powder, white wine, stock, and grated apple. Let simmer, covered, for 30 minutes.

3. Add yogurt and whisk, covered, until smooth.

4. In a large sauté pan, heat 2 Tbsp. of the olive oil and sauté chicken pieces until brown. Add to curry sauce and let cook an additional 10 minutes.

5. In the same sauté pan, add the remaining 2 Tbsp. olive oil and sauté the fruit over low heat until soft, about 8 minutes. Serve alongside the chicken curry.

Grilled Chimichurri Flank Steak

Grilling is a big part of traditional cooking; many people from around the world eat some form of grilled meat accompanied by a sauce. In many cuisines, the meats are grilled in traditional ovens, such as a tandoor in India, or a spit in a wood-burning oven for shawarma in the Middle East. Also, the meats are typically seasoned with a simple herb or spice sauce, such as charmoula, chimichurri, pesto, or harissa. The spices and garlic in these sauces kill bacteria and add flavor to the meat.

Serves 6

½	cup extra-virgin olive oil
¼	cup white wine vinegar
2	Tbsp. maple sugar
2	cloves garlic
1	tsp. ground cumin
¼	cup tightly packed fresh oregano leaves
½	cup tightly packed fresh cilantro leaves
1	cup tightly packed fresh parsley leaves
1	tsp. sea salt
	Freshly ground black pepper to taste
3	lb. grass-fed flank steak

1. Purée olive oil, vinegar, sugar, garlic, cumin, oregano, cilantro, parsley, salt, and pepper in blender. Marinate steak in half of marinade for 1 hour, or overnight in the refrigerator.

2. Grill flank steak on high heat 4-6 minutes on each side. When grilling, place the meat at 10 o'clock and when grill marks have appeared, rotate it to 2 o'clock. Repeat on the other side. Let meat rest for 10 minutes.

3. Slice meat thinly against the grain and serve with remaining marinade.

Bison and Dark Beer Chili

Bison meat is a leaner alternative to beef and it is usually not factory-farmed, which is why I like to use it for this recipe. I also like to use aduki beans instead of kidney beans because they are easier to digest. The small red aduki (sometimes spelled "adzuki") beans can be found in most specialty food stores or health food stores. I like to serve this dish with Cornbread (see recipe on p. 150).

Serves 6

1	cup aduki beans, soaked overnight and drained
2	Tbsp. extra-virgin olive oil
2	large onions, diced
2	red bell peppers, diced
2	yellow bell peppers, diced
1	jalapeño, chopped
2	lb. ground bison meat
1	Tbsp. ground cumin
½	Tbsp. ground coriander
2	Tbsp. chili powder
1	tsp. chipotle chiles in adobo, minced
3	cups crushed tomatoes
1	cup dark beer
1	tsp. sea salt
	Freshly ground black pepper to taste

1. Put the beans in a medium pot with cold water to cover. Bring to a boil, reduce heat, and cook beans until tender, 45 minutes to 1 hour.

2. Heat olive oil in large skillet over medium-high heat. Add onions and peppers. Sauté until vegetables begin to soften, about 15 minutes.

3. Add bison and cook until no longer pink.

4. Mix in cumin, coriander, chili powder, and chipotle chiles. Add tomatoes, beans, and beer. Bring chili to boil, stirring occasionally. Reduce heat and simmer 20 minutes, stirring often. Season with salt and pepper and serve.

Cornbread

This delicious and simple bread, pictured on p. 182 accompanying the Vegetarian Chili with Aduki Beans, makes a healthy side dish to any hearty chili.

Makes 16 pieces

½	cup butter, melted and cooled; more softened for the pan
1	cup corn flour (or stone-ground cornmeal)
¾	cup millet flour
⅓	cup maple sugar
1	tsp. salt
2	tsp. aluminum-free baking powder
2	eggs
1	cup buttermilk
½	cup grated Cheddar
1	jalapeño, seeded and chopped (optional)

1. Preheat oven to 350°F. Butter a glass 8x8-in. baking pan.

2. Combine corn flour, millet flour, sugar, salt, and baking powder in a medium bowl.

3. Crack the eggs into a medium bowl, add melted butter and buttermilk, and whisk to combine.

4. Make a well in the dry ingredients, pour liquid ingredients into the well, and whisk until well combined. Stir in Cheddar and jalapeño (if using).

5. Bake 30 minutes, or until a sharp knife inserted in the center comes out clean.

Grilled Fish with Cilantro Sauce

This is a very easy dish with Moroccan flavors. It goes well with Couscous (see recipe on p. 187) and Moroccan Carrot Salad (see recipe on p. 236).

Serves 6

1½	cups tightly packed fresh cilantro leaves
½	cup extra-virgin olive oil
¼	cup fresh lemon juice
2	cloves garlic
1	tsp. ground coriander
1	tsp. ground cumin
½	tsp. ground cardamom
½	tsp. ground ginger
1	tsp. sea salt
	Freshly ground black pepper to taste
2	lb. thick fish fillets, such as halibut, wild striped bass, or flounder

1. To make the marinade, combine cilantro, olive oil, lemon juice, garlic, coriander, cumin, cardamom, ginger, salt, and pepper in a blender and blend to a smooth paste.

2. Cover fish with marinade and refrigerate for 1-3 hours.

3. On a barbecue, grill fish 4-5 minutes per side.

4. Alternatively, roast the fish in an oven heated to 400°F for 6-8 minutes.

French Fish Stew (Bouillabaisse)

Traditionally, bouillabaisse was made with all the remnants of fish: heads, tails, bones, etc. I have adapted the recipe and made it a little lighter. My children's favorite part of this dish is the rouille on toast.

Serves 6

½	lb. medium shrimp, unpeeled
½	cup extra-virgin olive oil
1	cup thinly sliced yellow onions
2-3	leeks (white parts only, 1 green leaf reserved for bouquet garni), thinly sliced
2	cloves garlic, minced
1	red pepper, diced
1	large tomato, chopped
4	ribs celery, diced
1	fennel bulb, cored and diced
1	bouquet garni (2 sprigs thyme, 2 sprigs parsley, 2 bay leaves, and 15 peppercorns, wrapped in a leek leaf and tied together with twine)
	Zest of half an orange, about 2 tsp.
3	lb. red snapper, halibut, or any firm white fish
½	tsp. saffron
2	tsp. sea salt
¼	tsp. freshly ground black pepper
1	cup shrimp stock
2	Tbsp. lemon juice
⅔	cup Pernod
	Slices of French bread, toasted
	Rouille (see recipe on opposite page)

1. Peel and devein shrimp. Put shrimp peels in a small saucepan and add 2 cups water. Bring to a boil and boil for 10 minutes. Strain and reserve shrimp broth.

2. Heat ¼ cup of the olive oil in a large pan. When it is hot, add onions and leeks. Sauté for a minute, then add garlic and red pepper. Add tomato, celery, and fennel and stir well. Add remaining ¼ cup of olive oil, the bouquet garni, and the orange zest. Cook until the onion is soft and golden but not brown, about 6 minutes.

3. Cut fish fillets into 2-in. pieces. Add the pieces of fish and 2 cups of water to the vegetable mixture. Bring to a boil, then reduce heat and simmer, uncovered, for about 10 minutes. Add shrimp.

4. Add saffron, salt, and pepper. Add shrimp broth, lemon juice, and Pernod. Bring to a simmer again and cook, covered, about 5 minutes longer.

5. Serve with toasted slices of French bread and Rouille.

Rouille

Rouille is essentially a spicy mayonnaise. In fact, if you omit the saffron and red chile, you have homemade mayonnaise. My youngest child, who is the queen of condiments, loves to dip asparagus or artichokes in homemade mayonnaise.

Makes 1-1½ cups

4	cloves garlic, peeled
1	tsp. sea salt
½	tsp. ground red chile
	Pinch of saffron threads
½	tsp. Dijon mustard
1	large egg yolk
⅛	tsp. freshly ground black pepper
1	cup extra-virgin olive oil

1. In a large mortar, crush the garlic, salt, red chile, and saffron with the pestle.

2. Add the mustard, egg yolk, and pepper and mix well.

3. Gradually add olive oil, whisking continuously in the same direction until mixture thickens to consistency of mayonnaise.

Grilled Lamb Loin with Salsa Verde

This is one of my favorite summer dishes. The mix of herbs is so refreshing. I like to serve it with a simple green salad or sautéed summer vegetables.

Serves 6

1	cup extra-virgin olive oil
½	cup fresh lemon juice
½	cup scallions, sliced into thin rounds
½	cup chopped fresh parsley
¼	cup chopped fresh mint
¼	cup chopped capers
¼	cup lemon zest, from about 2 lemons
1	tsp. ground roasted cumin
	Pinch of red pepper flakes
1	Tbsp. sea salt
1½	tsp. freshly ground black pepper
3	lb. lamb loin (4-6 pieces)
1	tsp. chopped garlic

1. Make salsa verde by combining olive oil, lemon juice, scallions, parsley, mint, capers, lemon zest, cumin, red pepper flakes, 1 tsp. of the salt, and ½ tsp. of the pepper in a small bowl. Set aside.

2. Place the lamb loins in a large dish and rub the remaining 2 tsp. salt, 1 tsp. pepper, and the garlic all over them. Marinate at room temperature for 1 hour or overnight in the refrigerator.

3. Heat a barbecue. Grill the lamb, over medium heat, for about 5-6 minutes on each side, depending on the size of the steaks. When grilling, place the meat at 10 o'clock and when grill marks have appeared, rotate it to 2 o'clock. Repeat the same procedure on the other side.

4. Transfer the lamb to a plate and let it rest for 10 minutes.

5. Alternatively, you may roast the lamb for 4-5 minutes per side in an oven heated to 400°F. Let the meat rest for 10 minutes before slicing.

6. Serve lamb with the salsa verde.

Maple Spiced Barbecue Chicken

In summer, I love to make barbecue chicken with sautéed vegetables. It is just the right combination of sweet and spicy flavors.

Serves 6

3	lb. chicken thighs and drumsticks

For the dry rub

1½	Tbsp. sea salt
1½	Tbsp. paprika
1½	Tbsp. maple sugar
1½	Tbsp. ground mustard
2	Tbsp. lemon zest
1	tsp. freshly ground black pepper
1½	tsp. crumbled bay leaves
9	cloves garlic, chopped

For the barbecue sauce

2	large yellow onions, grated
4	cloves garlic, chopped
4	Tbsp. Worcestershire sauce
8	oz. crushed tomatoes
4	Tbsp. maple syrup
2	dried red chiles
12	oz. dark beer, such as lager or ale
2	cups water
1	tsp. dry mustard
1	tsp. chili powder
1	tsp. ground cumin
1	tsp. sea salt
	Freshly ground pepper to taste
4	Tbsp. apple cider vinegar

1. Combine the dry rub ingredients. Rub the mixture over the chicken pieces and refrigerate for at least 1 hour or overnight.

2. Combine the barbecue sauce ingredients except for the vinegar, in a large pot. Bring to boil, then reduce the heat and simmer for 30-45 minutes, or until it thickens.

3. When the sauce is thick and flavorful, add the vinegar and cook for an additional 2 minutes.

4. Grill the chicken legs on the barbecue for about 20 minutes per side, depending on the size of the legs. (The chicken legs are done when the juices run clear.) About 5 minutes before the end, brush with the barbecue sauce and cook until the chicken chars lightly.

5. Serve with the remaining sauce.

Canard à l'Orange

My parents used to make this every year on Christmas Day. It's one of my favorite dishes. You can substitute chicken for duck, if duck is not your thing.

Serves 6

2	Tbsp. orange zest
2	Tbsp. fresh thyme
2	Tbsp. unsalted butter, softened
4-6	duck breasts
2	oranges, cut into eighths

Orange sauce

1	Tbsp. unsalted butter
1	Tbsp. maple sugar
2	Tbsp. kuzu root starch (this can be found in Japanese or specialty food stores)
2	Tbsp. Grand Marnier
	Juice of about 8 oranges

1. Rub orange zest, thyme, and butter over ducks. Tuck 2 orange wedges under the skin of each breast. Refrigerate and let sit for 1-2 hours.

2. Preheat oven to 450°F.

3. Roast duck breasts for 20-30 minutes, depending on the size of the breasts. You do not want to overcook the duck or it will taste like rubber.

4. Meanwhile, make the sauce. Melt butter and sugar in a saucepan. Let cook over low heat until mixture browns slightly, 3-4 minutes.

5. Add kuzu root starch and whisk continuously over low heat until sauce thickens.

6. Add Grand Marnier and orange juice and bring mixture to a simmer, whisking continuously until sauce is smooth and creamy.

7. Ladle some sauce over duck. Serve with Creamy Mashed Potatoes (*see recipe on p. 213*).

Grilled Fish with Lemon and Capers

You can easily substitute chicken fillets instead of fish for this recipe.

Serves 6

	Juice of ½ lemon, about 2 Tbsp.
4	Tbsp. extra-virgin olive oil
5	cloves garlic, chopped
1½	Tbsp. chopped capers
2	Tbsp. fresh basil or oregano, chopped
1	tsp. sea salt
	Freshly ground black pepper to taste
2	lb. thick white fish (such as halibut) or boneless chicken breasts

1. Combine lemon juice, olive oil, garlic, capers, basil, salt, and pepper in a small bowl. Mix well.

2. Pour over fish or chicken and let marinate at room temperature for 1 hour or overnight in the refrigerator.

3. Grill on barbecue for 3-4 minutes per side for fish or 7-8 minutes per side for chicken, more depending on the thickness of the fish or chicken.

4. Alternatively, broil the fish in the oven for 5-6 minutes per side or 8-10 minutes per side for chicken.

Tandoori Chicken

The red color on tandoori chicken comes from the clay oven (tandoor) that it is cooked in. Some people add red food coloring if they don't have a tandoor, but I prefer to enjoy the chicken without the red color. This dish can also be made with medium-large shrimp or small lamb chops instead of chicken.

Serves 6

3	lb. chicken legs
1	tsp. sea salt
	Juice of 1 lemon, about 4 Tbsp.
2	cups plain, full-fat yogurt
½	large yellow onion, cut into chunks
1	clove garlic
1	1-in. piece of fresh ginger
½	green chile
1	tsp. ajwain or dried thyme
2	tsp. garam masala

1. Spread chicken pieces on large platter. Sprinkle with salt and lemon juice and rub into chicken. Set aside for 20 minutes.

2. Combine yogurt, onion, garlic, ginger, green chile, ajwain or thyme, and garam masala in blender. Blend to a smooth paste. Cover chicken with marinade and refrigerate overnight.

3. Grill chicken legs on a barbecue for 20-25 minutes per side over low heat, turning every 7-10 minutes.

4. Serve with Cucumber Raita (*see recipe on p. 237*).

Grilled Chicken Satay

Candlenuts, which are key to this recipe, grow in the tropics and are typically used in Malaysian and Indonesian cuisine. A good substitute is macadamia nuts. Serve the Satay with Peanut Sauce (see recipe on opposite page).

Serves 6

4	stalks lemongrass, roughly sliced
2	red chiles, seeded
2	dried chiles, seeded
4	candlenuts or macadamia nuts
1	tsp. shrimp paste
15	shallots, peeled
1	tsp. sea salt
½	tsp. freshly ground black pepper
2	tsp. palm sugar
4	Tbsp. coconut oil
1	cup coconut milk
1½	lb. boneless chicken breast cutlet, cut into 1-in. pieces
2	Tbsp. sesame oil
1	cucumber, peeled and thinly sliced
1	red onion, thinly sliced

1. In a food processor, make the rempah, or spice paste, by combining lemongrass, chiles, candlenuts or macadamias, and shrimp paste, and processing until smooth. Transfer to a bowl.

2. Add shallots, salt, pepper, palm sugar, coconut oil, and coconut milk and mix well. Pour over chicken and marinate for 1 hour.

3. Thread the chicken onto skewers through the center of each piece. Brush with sesame oil.

4. Grill or broil in an oven heated to 450°F, turning and brushing with marinade halfway through, until chicken is browned and fully cooked, 10-15 minutes.

5. Garnish chicken satay with cucumber and onion.

Peanut Sauce

You can substitute unsalted organic peanut butter for ground peanuts. Use ¼ cup and instead of following step 1, just add peanut butter to spice paste at the end.

Makes 1 cup

¼	lb. peanuts, roasted and ground
1	cup water
4	shallots, peeled
2	cloves garlic, peeled
½	lemongrass stalk
4	dried red chiles
1	slice ginger or galangal
2	Tbsp. coconut or sesame oil
1½	tsp. sea salt
2	Tbsp. palm sugar
1	Tbsp. fresh lime juice

1. In a pan, combine peanuts and water and bring to a boil over low heat. Cook for 30 minutes, stirring frequently, until thick.

2. To make a spice paste, combine shallots, garlic, lemongrass, chiles, and ginger or galangal in a food processor and process until smooth.

3. Heat coconut or sesame oil and fry spice paste for 3-5 minutes, until oil separates from spice mixture. Add paste to peanuts, along with salt, palm sugar, and lime juice.

4. Bring to a boil, reduce heat, and simmer for 5-7 minutes. Cool to room temperature.

Baked Sole in Tomato-Caper Sauce

This is my backup recipe for when I have very little time to prepare dinner, because it's so quick to make and everyone likes it, including my fish-hating daughter.

Serves 6

3	Tbsp. extra-virgin olive oil
2	large yellow onions, thinly sliced
3	cloves garlic, chopped
2	tsp. fresh oregano
2	Tbsp. capers
2	cups crushed tomatoes
1	tsp. sea salt
	Freshly ground black pepper to taste
1½	lb. sole or tilapia fillets
1	lemon, thinly sliced

1. Preheat oven to 350°F.

2. Heat olive oil over medium heat in a sauté pan. Add onion and sauté until soft, 5-7 minutes.

3. Add garlic and sauté until lightly colored, 1 minute. Stir in oregano and capers.

4. Add crushed tomatoes, salt, and pepper. Lower heat to a simmer and let cook for 15 minutes.

5. Spread one quarter of tomato sauce on the bottom of a large baking dish.

6. Arrange fish in a single layer on top of sauce. Pour on remaining sauce.

7. Bake in oven for 10-15 minutes, or until fish is just done and opaque.

8. Serve with rice or boiled potatoes. Garnish with lemon.

Steamed Chinese Fish Fillets

In traditional Chinese medicine, fish is viewed as a very healthful food. While fish tends to be a cooling food, when it is paired with warming vegetables and herbs such as ginger and scallions, it is fully balanced. Serve with steamed rice.

Serves 6

6	cloves garlic, chopped
3	scallions, cut into 2-in. lengths
1	2-3 -in. piece of ginger, cut into julienne slices
3	Tbsp. salted black beans
3	Tbsp. tamari soy sauce
1	Tbsp. unrefined sesame oil
6	firm white fish fillets, such as striped bass
	Large cabbage leaves, washed and trimmed
1	cup snow peas, trimmed
4	carrots, cut on diagonal into ¼-in. slices
1	cup kai lan or baby bok choy

1. Combine garlic, scallions, ginger, black beans, soy sauce, and sesame oil in a bowl. Pour over fish and marinate for 1 hour.

2. Fill wok halfway with water and bring to boil over high heat.

3. Place bamboo steamer over wok and lay cabbage leaves on bottom of steamer. Place fish on cabbage leaves and pour marinade over fish.

4. Arrange vegetables in another tier of bamboo steamer and place over fish. Steam 10 minutes or until fish and vegetables are cooked through.

5. Serve fish with the vegetables.

Poached Salmon with Saffron Aïoli

Aïoli, like rouille, is essentially a flavored mayonnaise. It's delicious with steamed fish and vegetables such as cauliflower, broccoli, carrots, and fennel. You can also use cod instead of salmon.

Serves 6

8	cups water
2½	cups white wine
	Handful of parsley and tarragon sprigs
1	fennel bulb, roughly chopped
2	lb. wild salmon fillets
	Sea salt
	Freshly ground black pepper

1. Combine water, white wine, parsley, tarragon, and fennel in large pan and bring to boil. Season salmon with salt and pepper and add to liquid. Bring liquid to simmer and cover with parchment. Poach salmon for 6-8 minutes.

2. Meanwhile, prepare aïoli.

3. Serve salmon with aïoli.

Makes ½ cup

¼	tsp. saffron threads
2	Tbsp. boiling water
2	eggs yolks, at room temperature
3	cloves garlic, crushed to a paste
1½	Tbsp. white wine vinegar
2	cups extra-virgin olive oil, plus extra if needed
1	tsp. sea salt
	Freshly ground black pepper to taste
	Fresh lemon juice to taste

Saffron Aioli

1. Place saffron threads in cup and cover with boiling water.

2. Combine egg yolks, garlic, vinegar, and saffron water with threads in a large bowl.

3. Whisk until mixture is foamy.

4. Gradually add olive oil, whisking continuously until mixture thickens to consistency of mayonnaise.

5. Season with salt, pepper, and lemon juice.

Fish Baked with a White Wine Sauce

This is a very light and flavorful sauce that also works well with baked chicken.

Serves 6

2-3 shallots, chopped

2 Tbsp. unsalted butter plus 4 Tbsp. chilled and cut into small pieces

1 cup dry white wine, such as Sauvignon Blanc

Juice of 1 lemon

¼ cup chopped capers

4 cloves garlic, chopped

¼ cup chopped parsley or tarragon (optional)

2 lb. firm white fish fillets (halibut, cod, or barramundi) or boneless chicken breast fillets

1 tsp. sea salt

Freshly ground black pepper

1. Preheat oven to 350°F.

2. Sauté shallots in 2 Tbsp. of the butter until soft, about 3 minutes.

3. Add wine and boil to reduce by half.

4. Add lemon juice, capers, and garlic and cook one minute.

5. Stir in pieces of chilled butter one at a time and mix well. Add parsley or tarragon (if using). Season with salt and pepper.

6. Butter a baking dish and lay fish fillets or chicken in a glass baking dish and sprinkle with salt and pepper. Pour sauce over the fish.

7. Bake fish in an oven heated to 375°F for 10-20 minutes depending on the size of the fillets (the fish should be opaque). For chicken fillets, bake for 30-45 minutes, depending on the size of the fillets.

Roasted Beef Tenderloin with a Red Wine Sauce

This recipe is my backup for when I have a large group of people coming for dinner and very little time to prepare dinner. I like to serve it with Gratin Dauphinois (see recipe on p. 215).

Serves 6

2-3	shallots, chopped
10	Tbsp. unsalted butter
2	cups sliced mushrooms (optional)
2	cups red wine, such as Cabernet
3	cups Basic Chicken Stock (see recipe on p. 116) or beef stock
2	Tbsp. fresh thyme or 2 tsp. dried thyme
2	bay leaves
5	lb. beef tenderloin
1	tsp. sea salt
	Freshly ground black pepper to taste

1. Preheat oven to 450°F.

2. Sauté shallots in 2 Tbsp. of the butter until soft. Add mushrooms (if using).

3. Add red wine and boil to reduce by half, 8-10 minutes.

4. Add chicken or beef stock, thyme, and bay leaves and simmer for 20 minutes. Season with salt and pepper. When the beef is done cooking, add the juices to the sauce.

5. To thicken sauce, cut 4 Tbsp. of the butter into small pieces and stir them in, piece by piece.

6. Season beef tenderloin with salt and freshly ground pepper, and rub the remaining 4 Tbsp. butter all over it. Put it on a baking tray in oven and roast 10-15 minutes on top and another 10-15 on the bottom, for medium well. Let it rest for 10 minutes before serving.

GRAINS, BEANS & PASTA

WHILE MEATS AND FISH ARE COMPLETE PROTEINS;
rice and legumes (beans) lack the specific amino
acids that would make them a complete protein.
However, when combined, rice and legumes
do make a complete protein, which is why
so many cultures have some sort of rice and
bean dish as part of their cuisine.

Provençal Chicken and Rice

This dish is great served with a mixed green salad in warm or cold weather.

Serves 6

3	lb. chicken legs and thighs
1	tsp. sea salt
	Freshly ground black pepper to taste
3	Tbsp. extra-virgin olive oil
2	large onions, chopped
5-6	cloves garlic, chopped
2	green bell peppers, chopped
2	cups crushed tomatoes
	Pinch of crushed red pepper flakes
1½	cup long-grain rice
1½	cup Basic Chicken Stock (see recipe on p. 116)
½	cup water
1	cup black olives, such as Niçoise olives, pitted
½	cup thinly sliced basil leaves

1. Season the chicken with salt and pepper. Heat the olive oil in a large sauté pan, then add the chicken, skin side down.

2. Brown the chicken over high heat for 7 minutes. Lower the heat, turn the chicken, and continue browning for another 3 minutes. Remove from the pan.

3. Add the onion to the pan. Cook, stirring, for 3-4 minutes. Stir in the garlic, bell pepper, tomatoes, and crushed red pepper. Cook over medium-low heat, stirring often, for 10 minutes.

4. Return the chicken to the pan, skin side up, cover, and cook for 10 minutes more.

5. Sprinkle the rice in an even layer over the chicken and vegetables. Add chicken stock and water and bring to a boil. Lower heat to a simmer, cover pan, and continue cooking until the rice and chicken are tender, 15-20 minutes.

6. Five minutes before serving, stir in the olives and correct the seasoning. Garnish with basil.

Indian Chicken Biryani

This delightful Indian dish takes a while to make, so I like to serve it on special occasions. As a matter of fact, biryani originated in Persia and was served at grand banquets.

Serves 6

4	large yellow onions, peeled, 3 quartered and 1 thinly sliced
4	cloves garlic
1	2-in. piece of fresh ginger
10	cloves
20	peppercorns
12	cardamom pods
¼	tsp. ground cinnamon
1	tsp. ground coriander
1	tsp. ground cumin
1	tsp. poppy seeds
¼	tsp. ground mace
3	Tbsp. sea salt
	Juice of 1 lemon, about 4 Tbsp.
1	cup plain, full-fat yogurt
6	Tbsp. ghee
2	bay leaves
2	lb. chicken legs and breasts
13	cups water
2	cups Indian basmati rice
2	tsp. saffron, roasted, crumbled, and soaked in 2 Tbsp. warm milk
2	Tbsp. blanched raisins
2	Tbsp. blanched almonds

1. To make the marinade, put the 3 quartered onions, garlic, ginger, cloves, peppercorns, 8 cardamom pods, cinnamon, coriander, cumin, poppy seeds, mace, 2 Tbsp. of the salt, and lemon juice in a blender and blend at high speed to a smooth paste. Add yogurt and mix well.

2. Heat ghee over medium heat. When hot, add bay leaves. Fry for 15-20 seconds. Add the sliced onions and fry, stirring, for about 10 minutes until they are brown and crispy. Remove carefully with a slotted spoon. Reserve ghee and bay leaves. Mix half the fried onions with marinade. Pierce chicken pieces with a fork and place in bowl with marinade. Marinate for at least 2 hours (maximum 6 hours) in the refrigerator.

3. Preheat oven to 300°F.

4. After 2 hours, place contents of bowl in a heavy-bottomed pot. Bring slowly to a boil, cover, lower heat, and simmer for 15 minutes. Remove chicken pieces, place them in casserole or large baking dish and cover. Boil down marinade paste, stirring, until ½ cup is left. Spoon the paste over the chicken.

5. Bring the water and the remaining 1 Tbsp. of salt to boil in large pot and add the remaining rice. After it has come to boil again, cook 5 minutes, drain rice in a colander, then place on top of chicken in casserole. Pour saffron milk over the rice. Spoon out the onion-flavored ghee from pan and sprinkle along with bay leaves and the remaining 4 cardamom pods over rice. Cover dish with aluminum foil. Bake for 1 hour.

6. Meanwhile, fry raisins and almonds in reserved onion-flavored ghee until lightly browned.

7. Garnish biryani with fried onions, raisins, and almonds.

Millet Pilaf

You can substitute a grain you prefer when making pilaf — rice, millet, quinoa, or barley—and add carrots and peas.

Serves 6

4	Tbsp. unsalted butter
1	small yellow onion, diced
2	cups millet
4	cups Basic Chicken Stock (see recipe on p. 116) or vegetable stock
3	bay leaves
3	fresh thyme sprigs
1	tsp. sea salt
	Freshly ground black pepper to taste

1. Melt butter and sauté onion over low heat until translucent but not browned, about 4 minutes.

2. Add millet and stir to coat well with butter.

3. Add stock, bay leaves, thyme, salt, and pepper.

4. Bring to a boil. Cover and simmer for 20 minutes.

Indian Vegetable Pullao

It is interesting to note that the words "pilaf" and "paella" originated from the Indian word "pullao," which is a rice dish cooked with vegetables or meat.

Serves 6

2	cups basmati rice
4	Tbsp. ghee
1	tsp. cumin seeds
1	carrot, peeled and diced
1	cup frozen peas
1	cup green beans, cut into ½-in. pieces
1	tsp. sea salt
½	tsp. turmeric
1	tsp. ground cumin
1	tsp. ground coriander
	Pinch of cayenne
2	Tbsp. chopped fresh cilantro
1	tsp. grated fresh ginger
1	clove garlic, minced
2 ⅔	cups water

1. Cover rice with water and let soak for 30 minutes-1 hour. Drain and rinse.

2. Heat ghee in a heavy pot over medium heat. Add cumin seeds and let them sizzle for 5-6 seconds.

3. Add carrot, peas, and green beans and sauté for a minute. Turn heat to medium low and add rice, salt, turmeric, cumin, coriander, cayenne, cilantro, ginger, and garlic. Sauté for 2-3 minutes until everything is well coated with ghee.

4. Add water and bring to boil. Cover and cook over low heat for 25 minutes. Let sit, covered, for 5-10 minutes.

5. Serve immediately.

Barley Pilaf

The great thing about pilafs is that you can add pretty much whatever you want to them: raisins, nuts, and other vegetables.

Serves 6

2	Tbsp. unsalted butter
2	onions, finely chopped
1½	cups pearl barley
2	cups Basic Chicken Stock (see recipe on p. 116) or vegetable stock or water
1	bay leaf
2	carrots, peeled, cut into ¼-in. dice
1	red bell pepper, cut into ¼-in. dice
½	cup of ¼-in.-diced squash or pumpkin
	Sea salt
	Freshly ground black pepper to taste
1	Tbsp. grated lemon zest
¼	cup sunflower seeds

1. Melt butter in heavy-duty medium saucepan over medium heat. Add onion and sauté until it begins to soften, about 5 minutes.

2. Add barley and stir until well coated with butter, about 3 minutes.

3. Add stock or water and bay leaf. Bring to boil. Reduce heat to low, stir once, and cover. Cook until barley is almost tender, about 30 minutes.

4. Add carrots, red bell pepper, and squash or pumpkin. Cover and cook until vegetables are tender, about 6 minutes. Remove pilaf from heat and stir. Cover and let stand 10 minutes. Discard bay leaf.

5. Season with salt and pepper. Stir in lemon zest and garnish with sunflower seeds.

Mixed Vegetable Paella

I like to make paella with just vegetables. Accompanied by a salad, it is a perfect summer meal.

Serves 6

4	Tbsp. extra-virgin olive oil
1	green chile, seeded and chopped
1	large yellow onion, thinly sliced
1	red bell pepper, thinly sliced
1	green bell pepper, thinly sliced
2	medium zucchini, medium-diced
4	vine tomatoes, peeled, seeded, and chopped
2	cloves garlic, minced
2	Tbsp. thinly sliced fresh basil leaves
2	tsp. smoked paprika
	Sea salt and freshly ground black pepper to taste
1½	cups Arborio rice
2	cups Basic Chicken Stock (see recipe on p. 116) or vegetable stock or water
2	Tbsp. chopped fresh parsley

1. Heat olive oil in a large sauté pan. Add chile, onion, and red and green peppers and sauté until soft, about 10 minutes.

2. Add zucchini, tomatoes, garlic, basil, paprika, salt, and pepper. Cover pan and simmer 10 minutes, until zucchini is soft.

3. Add rice and chicken stock, vegetable stock, or water. Bring to a boil. Lower heat, cover, and simmer for 20-25 minutes, until the rice is soft. Garnish with parsley.

Singaporean Chicken Rice

This is a classic dish in Singapore and is essentially chicken and rice cooked in chicken stock. I find it very simple yet flavorful. It looks long and complicated to make, but it's really not. The red chile sauce is very hot, so beware!

Serves 6

1	4-lb. chicken
3	tsp. sea salt
3	tsp. rice wine
2	scallions, halved and crushed
4	cilantro stems
6	slices fresh ginger, smashed
4	cloves garlic, smashed
1	lemongrass stalk
1	tsp. peppercorns
4	cups Chicken Stock (see recipe below)
2	tsp. light soy sauce
2	tsp. unrefined sesame oil
1	cucumber, thinly sliced on the diagonal

Makes 8 cups

1	small chicken
	Handful fresh cilantro (including stems)
1	large piece fresh ginger, smashed
5	cloves garlic, smashed
1	lemongrass stalk
3	slices galangal, crushed
4	"wild" lime leaves (kaffir)

1. Rub the whole chicken with salt and rice wine. Set aside for 15 minutes.

2. Put the scallions, cilantro, ginger, garlic, lemongrass, and peppercorns in the cavity of the chicken.

3. Combine 4 cups of chicken stock and 8 cups water in a large pot. Add chicken and bring to a boil. Boil for 30-40 minutes until chicken is cooked through.

5. Prepare rice (*see opposite page*).

6. Remove chicken to a plate, cut into small pieces, and glaze with soy sauce and sesame oil. Keep warm.

7. Put rice on plate and arrange chicken pieces on top. Serve with red chile sauce and garnish with cucumber.

Chicken Stock

1. Combine all ingredients in a large pot, cover with 8 cups water, and bring to a boil. Simmer for 1 hour, until chicken is fully cooked.

2. Reserve chicken for another use.

For the Rice

1½	cups long-grain rice
2	Tbsp. ghee
4	shallots, finely chopped
6	cloves garlic, finely chopped
1	1-in. piece fresh ginger, finely chopped
3	cups Chicken Stock (see recipe on opposite page)
1	tsp. sea salt
2	pandan leaves (optional)

For the Red Chile Sauce

8-10	long, red chile peppers, trimmed
1	1½-in. piece of fresh ginger, smashed
5	cloves garlic, peeled and smashed
¼	cup rice vinegar
1	tsp. sesame oil
1	Tbsp. lime juice
2	Tbsp. salt
1	tsp. palm sugar
2	Tbsp. chicken stock

Rice

1. Wash the rice and soak in water for 30 minutes; drain.

2. Heat the ghee in a pan. Sauté shallots, garlic, and ginger for 2 minutes. Add rice and sauté until it is fragrant.

3. Add chicken stock, salt, and pandan leaves (if using) and bring to a boil.

4. Lower heat, cover, and simmer for 30 minutes.

Red Chile Sauce

1. Combine all ingredients in a small blender and blend to a smooth paste.

Shrimp Paella

This is a simpler take on traditional paella, which includes mussels and squid.

2	Tbsp. extra-virgin olive oil
1	cup ½-in.-cubed ham
3	large yellow onions, diced
1	red bell pepper, diced
¼	tsp. saffron threads, crumbled
¼	tsp. smoked paprika
3½	cups Basic Chicken Stock (see recipe on p. 116), vegetable stock, or water
2	cups Arborio rice
1	tsp. sea salt
	Freshly ground black pepper to taste
1½	lb. medium shrimp (16-20 per pound), peeled and deveined
¼	cup pitted green olives
	Chopped fresh parsley, for garnish

1. Heat olive oil in heavy large skillet over medium-high heat. Add ham, onions, and red pepper. Sauté until golden-brown, about 8 minutes. Stir in saffron and paprika, then 3 cups of the stock and the rice.

2. Bring to boil, sprinkle with salt and pepper. Reduce heat to low, cover, and simmer until rice is almost tender, 15 minutes. Nestle shrimp into rice, top with olives, and drizzle with remaining stock to moisten.

3. Cover and cook until shrimp are opaque in center, 6 minutes.

4. Garnish with chopped parsley and serve.

Asparagus and Mushroom Risotto

Many cultures have some version of a rice dish cooked in a lot of water to make a savory porridge, which is very healing and warming for the body. The best thing about all these dishes is that there are nearly endless ways to create new versions by experimenting with a variety of ingredients.

Serves 6

5	Tbsp. unsalted butter, divided
¾	lb. button mushrooms, sliced
¾	lb. asparagus, cut on the diagonal into ½-in. pieces
1	tsp. sea salt
	Freshly ground black pepper to taste
5-6	cups Basic Chicken Stock (see recipe on p. 116) or vegetable stock or water
1	large yellow onion, chopped
1½	cups Arborio rice
½	cup dry white wine
1	cup grated Parmigiano-Reggiano cheese

1. Melt 2 Tbsp. of the butter in a sauté pan. Add mushrooms and sauté until lightly browned, about 4 minutes. Add asparagus and continue to sauté until just cooked. Season with salt and pepper.

2. Warm stock in a small saucepan.

3. Melt 2 Tbsp. of the butter in a medium saucepan. Add onion and sauté over low heat until soft (do not let the onion brown).

4. Add rice and cook 1 minute until it is coated with butter.

5. Add wine and cook over medium heat until absorbed, about 5 minutes.

6. Add 1 cup stock and cook over medium heat, stirring continuously, until absorbed. Repeat with remaining stock, adding ½ cup at a time, until rice is soft and creamy. This should take about 20 minutes.

7. Remove from heat. Mix in asparagus and mushrooms and last tablespoon of butter and sprinkle cheese on top. Season with more salt and pepper.

8. Let stand for 1 minute before serving.

Vegetarian Chili with Aduki Beans

This is a hearty dish, perfect for a winter's night. You can substitute with any type of beans in this recipe. I like to serve this with Cornbread (see recipe on p.150).

Serves 6

1	cup pinto beans, soaked overnight and drained
1	cup black-eyed peas, soaked overnight and drained
1	cup aduki beans, soaked overnight and drained
1	Tbsp. extra-virgin olive oil
1	large red onion, chopped into ¼-in. dice
2-4	cloves garlic, chopped
2	tsp. cumin seeds
2	Tbsp. chili powder
1	tsp. dried oregano
1	tsp. dried basil
½	tsp. ground cinnamon
2	bay leaves
1	jalapeño pepper, thinly sliced
1	red bell pepper, diced
2	celery ribs, diced
1	carrot, peeled and diced
2	cups water
1	cup chopped fresh cilantro
1	tsp. sea salt
	Freshly ground black pepper to taste

1. Put pinto beans, black-eyed peas, and aduki beans in separate medium pots with cold water to cover. Bring to a boil, reduce heat, and cook until tender, 45 minutes to 1 hour.

2. Heat olive oil in a large pan. Sauté onion and garlic for 2 minutes. Add cumin and continue to sauté 10 seconds. Add beans, remaining spices and herbs, jalapeño, red pepper, celery, and carrot and sauté an additional 2 minutes.

3. Add enough water to cover.

4. Cook uncovered over medium-low heat until vegetables are soft.

5. If desired, purée cupful of beans and vegetables and stir back into the dish.

6. Remove bay leaves and stir in the cilantro. Season with salt and pepper.

You can find aduki beans in most grocery stores.

Chickpea and Vegetable Tagine

Preserved lemons are essentially pickled lemons. The lemons are covered in a brine of water and salt and are left to ferment for several weeks. They are often called for in North African cuisine. You can find preserved lemons in specialty stores but, if they're unavailable, you can use regular lemons.

Serves 6

1	cup chickpeas, soaked overnight and drained
	Pinch saffron
2	Tbsp. extra virgin-olive oil
1	onion, chopped into ¼-in. dice
2	cloves garlic, sliced
2	tsp. ground cumin
½	cinnamon stick
¼	tsp. crushed red pepper
2	carrots, peeled and sliced into ½-in. rounds
2	sweet potatoes, cut into ½-in. cubes
2	cups butternut squash, peeled and cut into ½-in. cubes
2	cups crushed tomatoes
4	cups Basic Chicken Stock (see recipe on p. 116), vegetable stock, or water
1	preserved lemon, seeded and chopped
2	Tbsp. chopped fresh cilantro
1	tsp. sea salt
	Freshly ground black pepper to taste
	Couscous (see recipe on p.187)
	Harissa (see recipe on p.187)

1. Put the chickpeas in a medium pot with cold water to cover. Bring to a boil, reduce heat, and cook beans until tender, 45 minutes to 1 hour.

2. Soak the saffron in 2 Tbsp. warm water until ready to use.

3. Warm olive oil in large saucepan over medium heat. Add onion and garlic and cook until golden, about 5 minutes. Add cumin, cinnamon, and crushed red pepper and cook for an additional 2 minutes.

4. Add chickpeas, carrots, sweet potatoes, squash, saffron, tomatoes, and stock. Bring to a boil, lower heat, and simmer for 30 minutes, until vegetables are tender.

5. Add preserved lemon, cilantro, salt, and pepper and mix well.

6. Serve with couscous and harissa.

Harissa

Harissa is a red pepper paste added to flavor dishes. You can purchase it in specialty stores or make your own.

Makes 1 cup

2	smoked red chiles (such as chipotle), seeded and stemmed
4	dried red chiles (such as cascabel), seeded and stemmed
6	cloves garlic, peeled
2	tsp. ground coriander
2	tsp. ground cumin
½	tsp. ground caraway
1	tsp. sea salt
2	tsp. dried mint
4	Tbsp. chopped fresh cilantro
4	Tbsp. extra-virgin olive oil

1. Put dried chiles in a bowl and cover with hot water for 20 minutes. Drain.

2. Place chiles, garlic, coriander, cumin, caraway, salt, mint, cilantro, and olive oil in a blender and mix until smooth, adding more olive oil if necessary.

3. Harissa can be stored in a jar in the refrigerator for up to 1 month. Make sure that there is always oil covering the paste.

Couscous

Couscous is very simple to make and goes well with any stew. For variety and added flavor, cook the couscous in chicken or vegetable stock instead of water.

Serves 6

3	cups water
1½	cups whole wheat couscous
1	tsp. sea salt
1	tsp. unsalted butter

1. Bring water to a boil. Add couscous, sea salt, and butter.

2. Turn off heat and leave covered for 5 minutes. Fluff with a fork and serve.

Indian Chickpea Curry

When I first got engaged, I took my Indian mother-in-law aside and asked her for her recipes, which had been passed down from her grandmother, mother, and mother-in-law. Many of the steps were a little unclear. For example, they instructed to put a "pinch of this" or "handful of that" and, as a result, the food was inedible! Someone recommended some cookbooks by Madhur Jaffrey and they became my bibles. Since then, as my own cooking has changed, I have adapted the recipes. I am proud to say that my father-in-law thinks this is one of the better chickpea curries he has tasted.

Serves 6

2	cups chickpeas, soaked overnight and drained
2	medium onions, cut into ¼-in. dice
2½	tsp. sea salt
1	green chile, finely chopped
1	1-in. piece fresh ginger root, grated on a Microplane
	Juice of 1 lemon, about 4 Tbsp.
4	Tbsp. ghee
2	vine tomatoes, chopped
1	Tbsp. ground coriander
1	Tbsp. ground cumin
1	tsp. ground turmeric
2	Tbsp. garam masala
	Pinch cayenne pepper
2	cups water

1. Put the beans in a medium pot with cold water to cover. Bring to a boil, reduce heat, and cook beans until tender, 45 minutes to 1 hour. Drain.

2. Combine 2 Tbsp. of the onion, ½ tsp. of the salt, green chile, ginger, and lemon juice in a small bowl. (*Note: This is similar to the tarka used for dal.*)

3. Heat ghee in a large pot over medium heat. Sauté remaining onions until they start to brown, 6-7 minutes. Add tomatoes and sauté an additional 5 minutes.

4. Add the spices, remaining salt, chickpeas, and water. Mix well and bring to a simmer. Cover and let simmer for 15-20 minutes.

5. Add lemon juice mixture and stir to combine.

6. This dish is traditionally served with *bhattura*, a deep-fried puffy bread, but I prefer to serve it with plain rice.

Southwestern-Style Rice and Beans

I like to serve this dish with empanadas and guacamole (see recipe on p.113), but even a simple green salad will do.

Serves 6

4	cups kidney beans, soaked overnight and drained
3	Tbsp. extra-virgin olive oil
2	red onions, chopped
2	cloves garlic, chopped
1	green bell pepper, diced
1	Tbsp. chili powder
1	tsp. paprika
1	cup tomato sauce
¼	cup water
	Few dashes Tabasco sauce (optional)
4	cups cooked brown or white rice
8	oz. sour cream
2	Tbsp. lime juice
¼	cup chopped cilantro
½-1	tsp. salt

1. Put the beans in a medium pot with cold water to cover. Bring to a boil, reduce heat, and cook beans until tender, 45 minutes to 1 hour. Drain.

2. Heat the olive oil in a large sauté pan over medium heat. Add the onions, garlic, and green pepper and sauté until soft, about 10 minutes.

3. Add chili powder and paprika. Mix in tomato sauce, water, Tabasco (if using), and kidney beans and simmer for about 10 minutes, until mixture is hot and water has evaporated.

4. Mix in cooked rice. Simmer, covered, an additional 10 minutes until rice is hot.

5. Stir together the sour cream, lime juice, cilantro, and salt and serve with the rice and beans.

Traditional Lasagne Bolognese

Lasagne is a big treat in our household. It is the dish of choice for those celebrating birthdays and returning home from summer camp. While this version takes some time to make, it is also very delicious! The key is using quality ingredients.

Serves 6

For the bolognese sauce

3	Tbsp. extra-virgin olive oil
3	Tbsp. unsalted butter
½	onion, finely chopped
1	carrot, finely diced
1	celery rib, finely diced
1	lb. ground beef (I use ground round)
1	tsp. sea salt
1	cup dry white wine
½	cup organic, unhomogenized whole milk
¹/₈	tsp. freshly grated nutmeg
3	cups crushed tomatoes

For the béchamel sauce

3	cups organic, unhomogenized whole milk
6	Tbsp. unsalted butter
6	Tbsp. whole-wheat flour
1	tsp. sea salt
	White pepper to taste

For assembly

1	lb. lasagne sheets (I use whole wheat)
½	cup grated Parmigiano-Reggiano
2	Tbsp. unsalted butter

Make the bolognese sauce

1. Put the olive oil, butter, and onion in a heavy, deep saucepan over medium-high heat and sauté until the onion has turned a light golden color, about 3 minutes.

2. Add carrot and celery and continue sautéing until they begin to change color, about 5 minutes.

3. Add the beef, breaking it up with a wooden spoon. Add salt and cook, stirring occasionally, until the meat is just browned, 5-6 minutes.

4. Add the wine and cook, stirring occasionally, until it has completely evaporated, 10-15 minutes. Add the milk and the nutmeg and continue to cook, stirring, until most of the milk has evaporated, 10-15 minutes.

5. Add the tomatoes, stir, and once they start to bubble, turn the heat down very low. Simmer uncovered 1-1½ hours, stirring occasionally.

Make the béchamel sauce

1. Heat the milk until it just begins to bubble. Remove from heat.

2. Meanwhile, melt the butter in a heavy-bottomed saucepan over medium-low

CONTINUED >

Béchamel sauce is best when used the same day, but it keeps overnight in the refrigerator if necessary.

If you are using a no-boil pasta sheet, the lasagne will take longer to cook, so be sure to read the package for recommended cooking time.

heat. Add the flour, mixing with a wire whisk until smooth. Let the mixture cook for 1-2 minutes, stirring constantly, and being careful not to let it brown.

3. Begin adding the hot milk, a few tablespoons at a time, whisking the mixture smooth before adding more. When the consistency becomes thinner you can begin adding milk more rapidly. Continue until all the milk has been mixed in.

4. Cook over medium-low heat, stirring constantly with the whisk, until the sauce begins to thicken. The sauce is done when it coats the whisk thickly. Season with salt and white pepper before removing from heat.

Assemble the lasagne

1. Preheat the oven to 400°F. Cook pasta sheets in boiling water until just soft (about 4 minutes; check the package).

2. Smear the bottom a baking dish with some of the béchamel sauce and cover with a layer of pasta strips. Mix the rest of the béchamel with the meat sauce and spread a thin layer over the pasta.

3. Continue layering the pasta and the sauce until there are at least 5 layers. Save enough sauce to thinly cover the top layer of pasta. Sprinkle the grated cheese on top and dot with the butter.

4. Bake for about 40 minutes or until a light golden crust forms on top. Check by inserting a knife and testing that pasta is soft. Remove from the oven and allow to rest for 10 minutes before cutting and serving.

Pad Thai

This is another version of fried noodles that is very versatile. You can make this a vegetarian dish by omitting the shrimp and adding more vegetables. Alternatively, you can substitute chicken for the shrimp.

Serves 6

9	oz. rice noodles
3	Tbsp. unrefined sesame oil
3	cloves garlic, chopped
2	carrots, peeled and cut into matchsticks
2-3	celery ribs, trimmed and cut into matchsticks
1	Tbsp. palm sugar
3	Tbsp. Thai fish sauce
1	Tbsp. tomato paste
1	Tbsp. fresh lime juice
8	oz. medium shrimp (16-20 per pound), peeled, deveined
2	eggs, beaten
1	cup bean sprouts
2	scallions, thinly sliced
2	Tbsp. chopped fresh cilantro

1. Put the noodles in a bowl with hot water to cover. Let stand for 15 minutes. Drain.

2. Heat the oil in a large wok or sauté pan. Add the garlic, carrots, celery, palm sugar, fish sauce, tomato paste, and lime juice and stir-fry for 4 minutes.

3. Add the shrimp and stir-fry for 2 minutes.

4. Add the eggs and stir-fry until cooked.

5. Stir in the noodles and bean sprouts and stir-fry for an additional minute. Garnish with scallions and cilantro.

Singaporean Laksa Noodles

If there is a Chinatown or Chinese market close to where you live, you may be able to find ingredients like laksa leaves, candlenuts, or galangal. Otherwise, you can easily substitute other ingredients such as mint, cilantro, macadamia nuts, and fresh ginger. This is a very rich noodle soup with shrimp.

Serves 6

For the spice paste

1	1-in. piece turmeric root, peeled
½	cups peeled and sliced galangal or fresh ginger
5	dried chiles
1	fresh red chile
6	candlenuts or macadamia nuts, crushed
2	Tbsp. belacan (Malaysian shrimp paste)
1	Tbsp. ground coriander

For the noodles

1	lb. medium shrimp (16-20 per pound), peeled and deveined (reserve shells)
4	Tbsp. coconut oil
2	stalks lemongrass, smashed
2	cups coconut milk
2	cups beansprouts, blanched for 2 minutes and drained
2	lb. package rice vermicelli, cooked
	Laksa leaves, finely sliced (you can substitute ½ mint and ½ cilantro leaves)

1. For the spice paste, combine the ingredients in a food processor and grind to a smooth paste. If necessary, add water to make sure the paste is very smooth.

2. Steam shrimp for 5-7 minutes, until fully cooked.

3. Make a shrimp stock using 2 cups water and shrimp shells. Boil for 10 minutes and strain.

4. Heat coconut oil in a large pot. Fry spice paste and lemongrass until oil separates and lemongrass is fragrant.

5. Add coconut milk and shrimp stock and bring to a boil.

6. Put beansprouts and noodles in individual bowls. Add hot soup and garnish with shrimp and laksa leaves.

Vietnamese Pho with Beef

I discovered this dish while traveling in Vietnam. At first glance, this soup doesn't seem like much, but it is a delicious combination of flavors and substantial enough to be a meal in itself.

Serves 6

1	1-in. piece fresh ginger, peeled
1	shallot, peeled
6	cups Basic Chicken Stock (see recipe on p. 116) or vegetable stock or water
1	star anise
1	cardamom pod
2	Tbsp. Chinese chives, thinly sliced (these can be found in most Chinese markets)
2	scallions, chopped
1	large yellow onion, thinly sliced
6	oz. beef filet, sliced into thin strips
1	lb. dried rice noodles
	Cilantro, bean sprouts, thinly sliced red chiles, and lime wedges for garnish

For the nuoc cham sauce

4	cloves garlic, finely chopped
2	red chiles, finely chopped
¼	cup palm sugar
	Juice of 2 limes
½	cup fish sauce
1	cup water

1. Wrap ginger and shallot in foil and roast in an oven heated to 350°F for 20 minutes. Chop finely.

2. Combine chicken stock, ginger, shallot, star anise, and cardamom in a large pot. Bring to a boil and simmer for 30 minutes.

3. Remove star anise and cardamom. Add chives, scallions, and onion. Add meat to stock and let cook for 2 minutes.

4. Put rice noodles in boiling water and cook 2-4 minutes until fully cooked. Ladle noodles into bowls and then ladle soup on top.

5. Garnish soup with cilantro, bean sprouts, thinly sliced red chiles, and lime wedges.

Nuoc cham sauce

1. Combine all ingredients and serve as an accompaniment.

Cold Soba Noodles

Soba noodles are made of buckwheat, which is actually not related to wheat but to rhubarb. Cold soba noodles are eaten with a flavored broth. They are typically eaten in summer and are very cooling. This recipe is also delicious served with a piece of grilled salmon.

Serves 6

For the dipping sauce

¼	cup Mirin
¼	cup maple sugar
1	cup tamari soy sauce
1	3-in. piece of kombu seaweed
¼	cup bonito flakes
3	cups water

For the noodles

1	lb. soba noodles
¼	cup thinly sliced scallions
	Shredded nori seaweed
	Wasabi paste

Make the dipping sauce

1. Bring mirin to a boil and let simmer 5 minutes. Add sugar and simmer until dissolved. Add soy sauce and bring sauce to a simmer. Take off the heat as soon as it boils. Let cool.

2. Make the stock (dashi): Soak the piece of dried kombu seaweed in 4 cups water for about 20 minutes. Bring the mixture to a boil, then add the bonito flakes. Take off the heat and let sit for 5 minutes. Strain and reserve liquid, should be about 2-3 cups.

3. Add the dashi to the first sauce a little at a time, starting with 1½ cups, and bring to a simmer. Simmer for 2-3 minutes, then let cool.

Make the noodles

1. Cook soba noodles according to package directions. Alternatively, put noodles in a pot of boiling water. Do not return water to the boil. Cook for 7-8 minutes.

2. Drain the noodles and put in a bowl of cold water. Wash until noodles are no longer starchy. Set aside.

3. Put sauce in individual bowls and add scallions, nori, and wasabi. Put a handful of noodles in and serve.

VEGETABLES

IN MOST TRADITIONAL CULTURES, VEGETABLES ARE
an essential part of the cuisine. The simplest
way to cook vegetables is to find a combination
that you like and then sauté in extra-virgin olive oil.
Eating vegetables that are in season is also
important because you are getting them when
they have the most flavor.

Sautéed Summer Vegetables with Cilantro

This is delicious served with simply grilled fish or lamb. It is very light and the colors always make me happy.

Serves 6

¼	cup extra-virgin olive oil
1	red onion, cut into ¼-in. dice
1	red bell pepper, cut into ¼-in. dice
2	zucchini, cut into ¼-in. dice
1	yellow squash, cut into ¼-in. dice
2	ears of corn, kernels removed
1	tsp. sea salt
	Freshly ground black pepper to taste
2-3	dashes Tabasco sauce (or to taste)
¼	cup chopped fresh cilantro

1. Heat olive oil in a large sauté pan. Sauté onion until soft. Add red pepper and continue sautéing until it is soft, 3-5 minutes.

2. Add zucchini, yellow squash, and corn kernels and sauté an additional 3 minutes.

3. Season with salt and pepper, and Tabasco and garnish with cilantro.

Ragout of Potatoes, Carrots, and Snap Peas

Another yummy vegetable combination, which goes nicely with Baked Sole in Tomato-Caper Sauce (see recipe on p. 165).

Serves 6

¼	cup extra-virgin olive oil
1	red onion, thinly sliced
1	lb. new potatoes, sliced into ¼-in. rounds
½	lb. carrots, cut into ¼-in. rounds
2-3	Tbsp. vegetable stock or water, as needed
½	lb. snap peas (snow peas or green beans are also suitable), trimmed and halved
1	tsp. sea salt
	Freshly ground black pepper to taste

1. Heat olive oil in a large sauté pan. Sauté onion until softened, 3-5 minutes.

2. Add potatoes and carrots and sauté lightly; then cover pan to allow them to cook. If mixture is dry, add 2-3 Tbsp. stock or water. Potatoes and carrots should take 10-15 minutes to cook. Pierce a few pieces with the tip of a paring knife to test for doneness.

3. When potatoes and carrots are almost cooked, add snap peas and cook an additional 5 minutes, until they are just done.

4. Season with salt and pepper.

Sweet and Savory Roasted Vegetables

I am including this recipe in the Vegetables section because I love to add fruit to my savory dishes—whether it is raisins, apples, apricots, pears, or pineapples.

Serves 6

1	onion, sliced
2	red bell peppers, diced
1	pineapple, cut into 1-in. pieces
1	plantain, sliced (optional)
1	Tbsp. extra-virgin olive oil
1	Tbsp. grade B maple syrup
1	tsp. sea salt
	Freshly ground black pepper to taste
	Juice of 1 lime or lemon
1	Tbsp. unsweetened shredded coconut

1. Heat oven to 400°F.

2. Put onion, red peppers, pineapple, and plantain (if using) in a baking dish. Drizzle with olive oil and maple syrup, and season with salt and pepper. Toss well.

3. Roast for 30 minutes, or until vegetables are soft, tossing occasionally.

4. Remove from oven, toss with lime or lemon juice, then sprinkle with coconut.

Spring Vegetable Ragout

I really like the combination of asparagus and mushrooms. Both are rich in antioxidants and have been found to help prevent cancer tumors.

Serves 6

¼	cup extra-virgin olive oil
4-6	shallots, sliced
¾	lb. button mushrooms, sliced
1	tsp. sea salt, plus more to taste
	Freshly ground black pepper to taste
¾	lb. asparagus, cut into 1-in. lengths

1. Heat olive oil in a large sauté pan. Sauté shallots until soft, about 3 minutes.

2. Add mushrooms and season with salt and pepper. Cook 5 minutes. If mushrooms release a lot of liquid, allow some of the liquid to boil off before adding asparagus.

3. Add asparagus and sauté an additional 5 minutes. If asparagus are large, cover pan and let cook an additional 5 minutes.

4. Season with more salt and pepper.

Indian-Style Cauliflower with Potatoes

This dish is typically made in a karhai, *which is the Indian version of a wok. It is essentially a large sauté pan.*

Serves 6

1	head cauliflower, about 1lb., cut into bite-size florets
4	Tbsp. ghee
1	tsp. cumin seeds
2	medium potatoes, boiled, peeled, and cut into ½-in. cubes
1	tsp. ground cumin
½	tsp. ground coriander
¼	tsp. ground turmeric
½	green chile, seeded and chopped
½	tsp. ground, roasted cumin seeds
1	tsp. sea salt
	Freshly ground black pepper to taste

1. Soak cauliflower in water for 30 minutes. Drain.

2. Heat the ghee in a wide sauté pan, such as a wok or *karhai*. When hot, add the cumin seeds.

3. As soon as the seeds sizzle, add the cauliflower and stir for a few minutes until the cauliflower is browned. Lower the heat and cover the pot. Let the cauliflower cook for 7-8 minutes, until soft but not mushy.

4. Uncover the pot and mix in the potatoes and remaining spices. Stir to mix until the potatoes are heated through, 2-3 minutes.

Choucroute Garnie (Sauerkraut)

Fermented cabbage is a classic winter food. Not only is it delicious, but it is very good for you. Fermented cabbage has a lot of beneficial bacteria (also called probiotics) that help support your immune system. Another version of fermented cabbage is Korean kimchi *or Japanese* tsukemono.

Serves 6

2	lb. store-bought unpasteurized sauerkraut (try to buy fresh or raw sauerkraut)
2	Tbsp. extra-virgin olive oil
	Water to cover
1	cup dry white wine
1	apple, peeled and cubed
3	juniper berries
4	sausages (such as bratwurst or other German sausage)
1	small (¼ lb.) ham hock or 2-3 thick slices of Kassler ham
	Boiled or sautéed potatoes, for serving

1. Rinse sauerkraut.

2. Sauté sauerkraut in olive oil for 2 minutes. Add water, wine, apple, and juniper berries. The sauerkraut should be covered with the liquid. Let cook for about 20 minutes, uncovered.

3. Add sausages and ham and let simmer, covered, for another 15-20 minutes, until meats are cooked through.

4. Serve with potatoes.

Cabbage with Peas and Carrots

This is another super-easy Indian dish that I like to make. It goes well with everything, from Tandoori Chicken (see recipe on p. 160) to Cucumber Raita (see recipe on p. 237).

Serves 6

1	small head yellow cabbage, about 1lb.
4	Tbsp. ghee
2	tsp. cumin seeds
2	bay leaves
1	large or 2 small carrots, peeled and diced
10	oz. frozen peas
¼	tsp. turmeric
1	green chile, seeded and chopped
1	tsp. maple sugar
¼	tsp. garam masala

1. Core and shred the cabbage.

2. Heat the ghee in a large sauté pan over medium heat. When hot, add the cumin seeds and bay leaves.

3. As soon as the seeds sizzle, add the cabbage, carrots, and peas. Stir until the vegetables are coated with ghee.

4. Add the turmeric, chile, and maple sugar. Lower the heat, cover the pot, and cook for 8-10 minutes, until cabbage is wilted.

5. Sprinkle with garam masala.

Summery Ratatouille

As a child, I never liked ratatouille. One summer, not long ago, we got a ton of eggplants in our farm share and I had to find different ways to cook it. So, I decided to give ratatouille a second chance. I adapted this recipe from Nancy Harmon Jenkins's The Mediterranean Diet Cookbook. *I have changed some ingredients and simplified the process.*

Serves 6

1½	lb. regular eggplant
3	Tbsp. sea salt, plus more to taste
1½	lb. red bell peppers
½	cup extra-virgin olive oil
3	large yellow onions, chopped
2	cloves garlic, chopped
1½	lb. zucchini, sliced into ¼-in. rounds
1½	lb. tomatoes, peeled and chopped
½	tsp. maple sugar
1	tsp. ground coriander
¼	cup chopped fresh basil
¼	cup black olives, pitted
	Freshly ground black pepper to taste

1. Rinse eggplant and cut into 1½-in. cubes. Place cubes in a bowl and add salt and water to cover. Put a plate inside bowl with a weight so that the eggplant stays submerged. Set aside for about 1 hour. Drain and pat dry.

2. Preheat oven to 450°F. Put the peppers on an oiled baking sheet and roast until skin is dark and loose. Put peppers in a large bowl and cover with plastic wrap. Peel and seed peppers, then cut into long strips. Place in a large bowl with juices.

3. Heat the olive oil in a sauté pan over medium-low heat and add onions and garlic. Cook until onions are soft and golden, about 7 minutes.

4. Add eggplant and sauté over medium heat until it starts to brown.

5. Add zucchini and sauté until zucchini is soft and browns slightly.

6. Add red peppers and tomatoes. Lower heat and stir in maple sugar and coriander. Simmer until sauce thickens, about 15 minutes.

7. Stir in basil and olives, and season with salt and pepper.

Eggplant Bharta

This is the Indian version of ratatouille and has a little more kick than the Summery Ratatouille (see recipe on p. 211). This is usually served with plain chapatti or naan.

Serves 6

2	medium eggplant
1	onion, peeled and quartered
1	1-in piece fresh ginger
2	cloves garlic, peeled
3	Tbsp. ghee
½	tsp. turmeric
½	green serrano chile, thinly sliced
3	medium tomatoes, diced
1	tsp. sea salt
1	tsp. fresh lemon juice
1	tsp. garam masala
2	Tbsp. coarsely chopped fresh cilantro

1. Put the eggplant on a grill or direct flame. Turn it until just blackened on all sides.

2. Once the eggplant is "smoked," put it in a bowl and cover with plastic wrap. When cool enough to handle, peel the skin off. Chop the eggplant into 1-in. pieces.

3. Put the onion, ginger, and garlic in a blender with 1 Tbsp. of water and blend to a paste.

4. Heat the ghee in a large sauté pan over medium heat. While heating, pour in the paste from the blender and add the turmeric and green chile.

5. Add the chopped tomatoes. Lower the heat and cook for 10 minutes, stirring occasionally, until the mixture becomes a thick sauce.

6. Add the eggplant, raise the heat to medium low and cook for an additional 10-15 minutes. Season with salt, lemon juice, and garam masala. Garnish with cilantro.

Creamy Mashed Potatoes

The secret to mashed potatoes is butter. There is no way around it. In many traditional French dishes, potatoes are paired with cream or cheese or both because this "maintains" the balance of the foods. As I mentioned before, nightshade vegetables, such as potatoes, contain alkaloids that tend to deplete the body of minerals, especially calcium. When you eat these vegetables with dairy products, the mineral balance in the body is restored.

Serves 6

2	Tbsp. extra-virgin olive oil
1	head of garlic, trimmed
8	Yukon Gold potatoes, peeled and cut into large cubes
6	Tbsp. unsalted butter
¼	cup heavy cream (optional)
1	tsp. sea salt
	Freshly ground black pepper to taste

1. Preheat oven to 350°F. Pour olive oil on aluminum foil and wrap garlic in foil. Roast for 30 minutes. When garlic is done, peel and reserve.

2. In large pot, cover the potatoes with cold water. Bring to a boil and let cook for 30 minutes, or until potatoes are fully cooked. Drain.

3. Meanwhile, put butter and heavy cream (if using) in a small saucepan and heat gently.

4. Add the butter, heavy cream, garlic, salt, and pepper to the potatoes and mash with a potato masher.

If you absolutely cannot use butter, ½-1 cup olive oil will suffice. Watercress leaves are a flavorful addition to this lighter version of the dish.

Gratin Dauphinois

Many would say that this is my signature dish. Along with lasagne, it is a family favorite.

Serves 6

8	medium Yukon Gold potatoes
1½	cups heavy cream
1½	cups Gruyère cheese
1½-2	tsp. sea salt
1½-2	tsp. freshly ground black pepper

1. Preheat the oven to 400°F.

2. Peel and cut the potatoes into ¼-in. slices. Place in a bowl of cold water.

3. Arrange the potato slices in a 9x5-in. baking dish or a medium round dish so they are slightly overlapping.

4. Pour ½ cup of the heavy cream over the potatoes and sprinkle with ½ cup of the Gruyère and ½ tsp. each of the salt and pepper.

5. Arrange a second layer of potatoes on top of first layer, pour ½ cup of the heavy cream and sprinkle with another ½ cup of Gruyère, salt, and pepper.

6. Continue layering until you have used all the potatoes, cream, and cheese.

7. Bake for 40 minutes, until top is browned and cream is bubbling. Test whether potatoes are fully cooked by inserting a paring knife into them. Gratin is done when potatoes are soft.

Sweet Potato Fries

For some strange reason, if I were to make these potatoes and call them roasted sweet potatoes, my children might not eat them. However, when I call them sweet potato fries, they devour them. So, sweet potato fries it is!

Serves 6

5	sweet potatoes, cut into wedges
½	cup extra-virgin olive oil
	Sea salt and freshly ground black pepper to taste
2	Tbsp. minced fresh parsley

1. Preheat oven to 350°F. In a bowl toss sweet potatoes with olive oil. Sprinkle with salt and pepper. Arrange potatoes in a single layer on a baking sheet.

2. Roast 30-45 minutes until soft and browned, turning once if necessary.

3. Garnish with parsley.

Cauliflower with Mustard-Lemon Butter

I love the combination of mustard, lemon, and capers because I feel it adds a nice kick to foods that may be a little boring. You can also combine cauliflower and broccoli in this recipe.

Serves 6

1	medium cauliflower, cut into bite-size florets
6	Tbsp. unsalted butter
2	Tbsp. fresh lemon juice
2	Tbsp. Dijon mustard
1½	tsp. grated lemon zest
1	tsp. sea salt
1	Tbsp. capers
1	Tbsp. chopped fresh parsley

1. Steam cauliflower in a large steamer until just tender, 5-7 minutes.

2. Meanwhile, melt butter in a small saucepan over medium heat. Whisk in lemon juice, mustard, lemon zest, salt, and capers.

3. Pour sauce over cauliflower and mix well. Garnish with chopped parsley.

Roasted Root Vegetables

Like many of the vegetable dishes presented in the previous pages, you can use any combination of vegetables you prefer in this dish. I sometimes like to add burdock root because it is so good for the digestive system. Root vegetables are said to be very grounding and warming.

Serves 6

2	sweet potatoes, cut into ¾-in. cubes
2	beets, cut into ¾-in. cubes
2	carrots, cut into ¾-in cubes
2	parsnips, cut into ¾-in. cubes
3	cloves garlic, minced
½	cup extra-virgin olive oil
1	tsp. sea salt
	Freshly ground black pepper to taste
2	Tbsp. minced fresh parsley

1. Preheat oven to 350°F. Combine sweet potatoes, beets, carrots, parsnips, and garlic in a bowl and mix with olive oil. Arrange vegetables in a single layer on a baking sheet. Roast for 45 minutes until soft.

2. Season with salt and pepper. Garnish with parsley.

SALADS

I HAVE EATEN SALAD EVERY DAY FOR AS LONG AS I CAN REMEMBER and now my family does, too. Although I am not an advocate of a purely raw food diet, I feel that it is important to incorporate salad greens into your diet, as they have lots of nutrients, vitamins, and minerals. Salads also aid digestion because they help the body eliminate wastes and toxins. Put simply, salads are an easy and tasty way to incorporate lots of vegetables into your diet.

Mom's Best Vinaigrette

For most of the salads I make, I use one simple dressing that my mother taught me. Here's the recipe.

Makes about ½ cup

1   Tbsp. vinegar (I like to use white balsamic, Champagne, white wine vinegar, or lemon juice)

½   tsp. Dijon mustard

¼   tsp. sea salt

   Freshly ground black pepper to taste

1   Tbsp. chopped herbs such as parsley or tarragon (optional)

1   Tbsp. chopped capers (optional)

1   chopped shallot (optional)

4-5   Tbsp. extra-virgin olive oil

1. Combine vinegar, mustard, salt, and pepper in a small bowl. Mix well.

2. If you are adding herbs, capers, or shallots add them here.

3. Add olive oil slowly, mixing as you go.

4. Drizzle over salad before serving.

You can also use walnut, hazelnut, or flaxseed oil, or a combination of olive oil and walnut/hazelnut/flaxseed oil.

Fennel Salad with Black Olives and Oranges

Fennel is a great digestive plant and herb, so I like to serve this salad after a heavy meal.

Serves 6

2	large fennel bulbs
2	oranges
1	cup pitted black Kalamata olives
¼	cup extra-virgin olive oil
	Pinch dried oregano
¼	tsp. sea salt
	Freshly ground black pepper to taste

1. Cut fennel in quarters, then lengthwise in slices.

2. Peel oranges, remove pith, and cut into segments.

3. Mix fennel, oranges, and olives in a medium bowl. Season with oil, oregano, salt, and pepper.

Summer Chopped Salad

This salad has a lot of texture and can easily be served with just a piece of grilled meat or fish for a nice summer's meal.

Serves 6

1   cucumber, seeded and diced

2   ears of corn, cooked, and kernels cut off the cob

2   cups cherry tomatoes, halved

1   avocado, peeled, pitted, and cubed

2   Tbsp. chopped fresh cilantro

Mom's Best Vinaigrette (see recipe on p. 221), using lime juice instead of vinegar and 1 clove garlic, chopped

1. Combine cucumber, corn, tomatoes, avocado, and cilantro in a large bowl.

2. Toss with Mom's Best Vinaigrette.

Mâche Salad with Shallots and Green Beans

It's important to use green beans in season so they are crispy and slightly sweet. The shallots add an extra kick of flavor to this nicely crunchy salad. I also like to use asparagus instead of green beans.

Serves 6

½	lb. green beans, trimmed
¾	lb. mâche, washed
2	shallots, finely chopped
	Mom's Best Vinaigrette (see recipe on p. 221)

1. Cut green beans into 1-in. pieces. Place in a pot of boiling water and cook until just done, about 3 minutes. Plunge into a medium bowl of ice water. Remove and let dry.

2. Combine mâche, green beans, and shallots and toss with Mom's Best Vinaigrette.

Endive Salad with Blue Cheese and Walnuts

Like the Arugula Salad with Pears and Blue Cheese (see recipe on p. 233), this salad has a nice combination of bitter and salty ingredients. It is a very light and refreshing, perfect for a warm summer's day. This salad also goes well with finely chopped boiled eggs instead of blue cheese and walnuts.

Serves 6

5-6 endives, cut lengthwise into ¼-in. slices

¼ lb. blue cheese, crumbled

Handful of chopped walnuts (optional)

Mom's Best Vinaigrette (see recipe on p. 221), using lemon juice instead of vinegar

1. Combine endives, blue cheese, and walnuts (if using) in a large bowl.

2. Toss with Mom's Best Vinaigrette.

Salad in a Glass

Some salad greens, such as arugula and dandelion, are good cleansing greens. In spring, if I am feeling a little heavy from the winter or just want to cleanse my body, I make this green juice. If you make this in a blender, you should strain the juice before you drink it.

5	oz. arugula and/or dandelion greens, thoroughly rinsed and spun dry
1	cucumber, peeled
4-6	celery stalks, cleaned and trimmed
1	apple, seeded
	Handful parsley leaves
2-3	thin (¼ in.) slices of fresh ginger, peeled (optional)
	Mint sprig for garnish

1. Combine arugula and/or greens, cucumber, celery, apple, parsley, and ginger (if using) in a juicer or blender. Mix until smooth, about 2 minutes, pulsing regularly.

2. Garnish with a sprig of mint and serve.

Mesclun Salad with Cranberries, Walnuts, and Balsamic Vinaigrette

It is always nice to add some dried fruit to salads. This is a classic salad that is well received in both summer and winter.

Serves 6

¾ lb. mesclun salad, thoroughly rinsed and spun dry

¼ cup dried, unsweetened cranberries

¼ cup walnuts, chopped

½ cup goat cheese, sliced or cubed (optional)

Mom's Best Vinaigrette (see recipe on p. 221), using red balsamic vinegar

1. Combine mesclun, cranberries, walnuts, and goat cheese (if using) in a large bowl.

2. Toss with Mom's Best Vinaigrette.

Arugula Salad with Figs and Walnuts

I like to chew so I prefer this salad with dried figs for the added texture, but it can be made with fresh figs if you have them.

Serves 6

½   medium onion, thinly sliced

2   Tbsp. white wine vinegar

¾   lb. arugula, rinsed and spun dry

15   dried or fresh figs, sliced into ½-in. slices

¼   cup walnuts, coarsely chopped

Mom's Best Vinaigrette (see recipe on p. 221), using red balsamic vinegar and replacing the mustard with honey

1. Cover sliced onions with hot water and the vinegar. Soak onions for 20 minutes, then drain (no drying). This will macerate them, making their flavor less strong.

2. Combine arugula, onions, figs, and walnuts in a large bowl.

3. Toss with Mom's Best Vinaigrette.

Greek Salad

My kids love this salad, and because the lettuce is quite thick it can easily be packed for a school lunch without getting mushy. It goes very nicely with whole-wheat pita and hummus.

Serves 6

2	heads romaine lettuce, thoroughly rinsed and spun dry
½	lb. cherry tomatoes, halved
1	cucumber, peeled and cut into ¼-in. rounds
1	red onion, thinly sliced
1	green bell pepper, diced
½	cup pitted Kalamata olives
1	cup diced or crumbled feta cheese
2	tsp. chopped fresh oregano

For the dressing

2	Tbsp. red wine vinegar
½	tsp. mustard
¼	tsp. sea salt
	Freshly ground black pepper to taste
6	Tbsp. extra-virgin olive oil

1. Place the lettuce leaves in a salad bowl or on a platter. Arrange the tomatoes, cucumber, onion, bell pepper, olives, feta, and oregano over the lettuce.

2. For the dressing, combine the vinegar, mustard, salt, and pepper in a small bowl and mix well. Add olive oil and whisk until well combined.

3. Toss salad with dressing and serve.

Beet Salad

Beets are a great blood cleanser. They are also delicious and a warming winter vegetable. When you cook the beets, the skin should slip off very easily. If it doesn't, peel it with a paring knife.

Serves 6

4	large beets, tops removed
4	scallions, white parts only, thinly sliced
	Mom's Best Vinaigrette (see recipe on p. 221)

1. Cover beets with water in a medium pot and boil until soft, 1-1½ hours. Cool and then peel beets. Cut into cubes and put in a medium bowl.

2. Thinly slice scallions and add to beets.

3. Toss with Mom's Best Vinaigrette.

Arugula Salad with Pears and Blue Cheese

Pears and blue cheese make a great combination of sweet and salty. To keep the pear from oxidizing and turning brown, rub the cut surfaces with lemon juice. The vitamin C in lemon juice is an important antioxidant.

Serves 6

¾	lb. arugula
2	pears, peeled and thinly sliced
¼	lb. blue cheese, crumbled
	Handful of chopped walnuts (optional)
	Mom's Best Vinaigrette (see recipe on p. 221)

1. Combine arugula, pears, blue cheese, and walnuts (if using) in a large bowl.

2. Toss with Mom's Best Vinaigrette.

Indian Cabbage Salad

This is sort of an Indian version of cole slaw and is another very simple yet tasty salad to make.

Serves 6

2	cups cabbage, shredded
2	cups carrot, peeled and shredded
¼	cup extra-virgin olive oil or sesame oil
1	hot green chile, seeded and chopped
½	cup chopped fresh cilantro
½	tsp. maple sugar
2	Tbsp. lemon juice
¼	tsp. sea salt

1. Combine cabbage, carrot, olive oil, chile, cilantro, sugar, lemon juice, and salt in a large bowl.

2. Mix well and serve.

Moroccan Carrot Salad

This is a classic Moroccan salad which is super-easy to make and very tasty.

4-6	large carrots
1½	cups fresh orange juice
	Juice of one lemon, about 4 Tbsp.
1	tsp. honey
½	tsp. ground cumin (optional)
1	cup raisins
½	cup walnut halves

1. Peel and grate carrots. Stir in orange juice, lemon juice, honey, cumin (if using) and raisins. Marinate while preparing walnuts.

2. Preheat oven to 350°F. Spread walnut halves on ungreased cookie sheet and roast 10-15 minutes, until lightly browned.

3. Add to salad. Toss and serve.

Traditional Swiss Potato Salad

This recipe is adapted from the potato salad my mother made for the family when I was growing up. If you can't find Yukon Gold potatoes, look for any golden variety for the creamiest flavor.

9	medium Yukon Gold potatoes
1	small onion, chopped
3	dill pickles, cut into ¼-in. dice
	Mom's Best Vinaigrette (see recipe on p. 221), recipe doubled
½ -1	cup Basic Chicken Stock, warm (see recipe on p. 116)

1. Boil potatoes in their skins and let cool to room temperature. This is best done the day before.

2. Peel and cube potatoes and put in a medium bowl.

3. Add chopped onion and pickles.

4. Toss with Mom's Best Vinaigrette.

5. Just before serving, toss lightly with warm chicken stock.

Cucumber Raita

This is very similar to Greek taramasalata and is a good accompaniment to dishes that don't have much gravy, such as cauliflower with potatoes or tandoori chicken. In India, the cucumber is typically grated but I like to dice it into ½-in. squares so there is more crunch.

Serves 6

2	cups plain full-fat yogurt
1	large cucumber, peeled, seeded, and diced
2	Tbsp. finely slivered fresh mint, plus more for garnish (optional)
1	tsp. sea salt
½	tsp. ground roasted cumin seeds
	Pinch of paprika and cayenne

1. Mix yogurt in a medium bowl until smooth.

2. Add cucumber, mint (if using), salt, and cumin, and mix well.

3. Sprinkle with pinches of paprika and cayenne, garnish with fresh mint, and serve.

To roast cumin seeds, put them in a small pan over medium heat and dry roast until fragrant. Then grind in a spice grinder. Roasted spices are more generally more flavorful.

Lentil Salad with Carrots and Celery

This salad is a hearty dish that I often serve for lunch. It's important to wait 10-15 minutes before serving the salad so that the flavors have time to come together.

Serves 6

1½ cups French du Puy lentils, rinsed

2 tsp. sea salt

2 medium carrots, diced

1 large celery rib, diced

2 Tbsp. thinly sliced scallions, white parts only

2 Tbsp. chopped fresh parsley

1 red bell pepper, diced

¼ cup walnuts, chopped

For the dressing

1 cup organic whole-milk yogurt

2 Tbsp. fresh lemon juice

2 tsp. white wine vinegar

3 Tbsp. extra-virgin olive oil

Sea salt and freshly ground black pepper to taste

1. Bring 6 cups water to boil in a large pot. Add lentils and salt and boil 15-20 minutes. Drain and rinse under cold water.

2. Transfer lentils to serving bowl. Add remaining ingredients.

3. To make dressing, combine yogurt, lemon juice, vinegar, olive oil, salt, and pepper. Whisk until smooth. Pour dressing over salad and mix well. Let salad stand 10-15 minutes and then serve.

Vietnamese Green Papaya Salad

Green papaya is simply unripe papaya. When it is combined with carrots and herbs, it is very tasty.

Serves 6

½	green papaya, peeled, and grated/shredded
3	shallots, thinly sliced
¼	cup chopped fresh cilantro
½	cup chopped fresh mint
	Juice of 1 lime, about 3 Tbsp.
2	Tbsp. fish sauce
2	Tbsp. maple or palm sugar
2	Tbsp. unsalted roasted peanuts, (optional)
1	red chile, seeded and thinly sliced

1. Place papaya in a bowl of water for 10 minutes. Drain.

2. Mix papaya with shallots, cilantro, and mint. Add lime juice, fish sauce, and sugar and mix well.

3. Garnish with peanuts (if using) and red chile and serve.

Mixed Green Salad

This refreshing summer salad is virtually a daily dish in our house because it's an easy way for me to get some vegetables into my kids.

Serves 6

2	heads of lettuce, washed and dried (I prefer Boston lettuce)
1	cucumber, peeled, seeded and diced
1	pint cherry tomatoes, halved
1	carrot, peeled and thinly sliced
1	avocado, peeled, pitted and thinly sliced (optional)
	Mom's Best Vinaigrette (see recipe on p. 221)

1. Combine lettuce, cucumber, tomatoes, carrot, and avocado (if using) in a large bowl.

2. Toss with Mom's Best Vinaigrette just before serving.

White Bean and Vegetable Salad

The great thing about bean salads is that you can really mix whatever you want: white beans or chickpeas with herbs, white beans with cherry tomatoes and parsley, chickpeas with cherry tomatoes and cilantro, black beans with cherry tomatoes, red onions, and cilantro. If you don't like a particular bean, you can just substitute one that you prefer.

Serves 6

1	cup white beans (cannellini or navy), soaked overnight and drained
3	cloves garlic, minced
¼	cup Parmiggiano-Reggiano, grated
¼	cup fresh lemon juice
1	tsp. lemon zest
½	tsp. sea salt
	Freshly ground black pepper to taste
¼	cup extra-virgin olive oil
2	cups cherry tomatoes, halved
1/3	cup chopped parsley
1	sprig fresh rosemary, finely chopped, or 1 tsp. dried

1. Put beans in a medium pot with cold water to cover. Bring to a boil, reduce heat and cook until soft, 45 minutes to 1 hour.

2. Put garlic, cheese, lemon juice, and lemon zest in a blender or food processor and process until smooth. Season with salt and pepper.

3. Combine olive oil, tomatoes, parsley, rosemary, and the garlic and cheese mixture in a large bowl and mix well.

4. Add the beans to the bowl and stir gently to combine.

Southwestern Black Bean Salad

This salad is very nourishing and goes well with the Spiced Chicken Quesadillas (see recipe on p. 105).

(see recipe on p. 105).

Serves 6

½	cup black beans, soaked overnight and drained
1	red onion, diced
2	ears of corn, cooked and kernels cut off the cob
1	red bell pepper, diced
1	green or yellow bell pepper, diced
1	avocado, peeled, pitted, and diced
1	large cucumber, peeled and diced
½	cup chopped fresh cilantro

For the dressing

2	Tbsp. lime juice
1	clove garlic, chopped
¼	tsp. sea salt
	Freshly ground black pepper to taste
4	Tbsp. extra-virgin olive oil

1. Put the beans in a medium pot with cold water to cover. Bring to a boil, reduce heat, and cook until tender, 45 minutes to 1 hour.

2. Combine beans, onion, corn, peppers, avocado, cucumber, and cilantro in a large bowl.

3. Combine ingredients for dressing in a small bowl and mix well.

4. Pour dressing over beans and mix well.

Quinoa with Corn, Scallions, and Cilantro

This is another light and refreshing summer salad that goes well with grilled meat or fish.

Serves 6

1	cup quinoa, soaked over-night and drained
1	Tbsp. lemon zest
	Juice of 1 lemon, about 4 Tbsp.
2	Tbsp. unsalted butter, melted
1	Tbsp. honey
½	tsp. sea salt
	freshly ground black pepper to taste
3	ears of corn, cooked and kernels cut off the cob
3	scallions, thinly sliced, white and light-green part
1	red bell pepper, diced
¼	cup chopped fresh cilantro

1. Bring large pot of salted water to boil. Add quinoa, cover, and cook on medium heat until white dot of uncooked starch in center is gone, 11-14 minutes. Drain and spread on large plate to cool.

2. While quinoa is cooking, whisk together dressing of lemon zest and juice, butter, honey, salt, and pepper in a bowl until combined.

3. Put quinoa in a bowl with corn, scallions, pepper, and cilantro, and toss with dressing before serving.

 It is very important to soak quinoa overnight because it contains a lot of phytic acid, which can deplete calcium and other minerals from the body. Soaking the quinoa removes some of the acid.

Farro Salad

*The great thing **about grain salads** is that the grains can be interchanged for one another, **and you will** still get a great result. Some of the grains I like to use are farro, quinoa, **and bulgur.** Farro is a traditional wheat grain. It is rich and nutty, so it **gives a nice crunch** to the salad.*

Serves 6

1   lb. farro

¼   lb. arugula, **chopped**

1   large cucumber, **seeded** and chopped

1   pint cherry **tomatoes,** halved

1   large red onion, **sliced thin**

1   clove garlic, **chopped**

1   cup black **Kalamata olives,** halved

¼   cup fresh **parsley, thyme,** or oregano, or a **combina-**tion

       Mom's Best **Vinaigrette** (see recipe on p. 221), using red wine **vinegar**

1. Cook farro according to package instructions.

2. Drain and mix with arugula, cucumber, tomatoes, onion, garlic, olives, and parsley.

3. Toss well with Mom's Best Vinaigrette and serve.

Bulgur and Chickpea Salad

This is kind of a different take on tabouleh, which is a salad made of bulgur and herbs. I really like the texture of the salad.

Serves 6

1	cup chickpeas, soaked overnight and drained
1	cup coarse bulgur
1	large cucumber, seeded and diced
1	pint cherry tomatoes, halved
6	scallions, thinly sliced
¾	cup cilantro, chopped

For the dressing

6-8	Tbsp. extra-virgin olive oil
1½	tsp. lemon zest
2	Tbsp. lemon juice
3	Tbsp. organic yogurt
½	tsp. harissa (Moroccan red chile paste; see recipe on p. 187)
	Sea salt and freshly ground black pepper to taste

1. Put the chickpeas in a medium pot with cold water to cover. Bring to a boil, reduce heat, and cook chickpeas until tender, 45 minutes to 1 hour.

2. Bring 2 cups of salted water to a boil. Add bulgur and mix well. Cover, reduce heat to low and cook for 10-20 minutes (depending on coarseness of grain) until all the water is absorbed. Spread on a large plate to cool.

3. Combine chickpeas, bulgur, cucumber, tomatoes, scallions, and cilantro in a bowl.

4. Combine dressing ingredients in a blender and mix well. Pour over salad, mix well, and let sit for 10 minutes before serving.

Desserts

MY FAVORITE DESSERTS ARE are made with fruit. Fruit, like vegetables, have so many vitamins and minerals and are a great source of fiber. Not only that, but when you use fruit, you don't need to use as much sugar in the dessert. The best part about fruit desserts is that you can eat them for breakfast or snack!

Broiled Assorted Fruit

I love broiled fruit for dessert. My favorite fruit to use are bananas, pineapples, plums, and peaches. Another option is to sauté fruit slices in a little butter and maple sugar and, if desired, cinnamon, star anise and/or cardamom to give the dish a little kick. This is especially good with harder fruit, such as apples and pears.

Serves 6

6   ripe fruit, such as bananas (halved length-wise), pineapple slices, plum or peach wedges

½   cup unsalted butter, melted

½   cup water

½   cup maple sugar

1. Set the oven to broil. Butter a 9x5-in. glass baking dish.

2. Place fruit in baking dish and coat with melted butter.

3. Bring water and maple sugar to boil in a small pan. Pour over fruit.

4. Broil for 10-15 minutes, until browned and tender, turning once.

Sweet Potato Pudding Pie

I love this healthy, nourishing version of sweet potato pie. I also like to make this with banana instead of sweet potato.

Serves 6

1	cup raisins
2	Tbsp. rum
1	cup whole-wheat pastry flour or millet flour
½	tsp. grated nutmeg
½	tsp. sea salt
1	lb. sweet potatoes, cooked and mashed
3	large eggs
1	13-oz. can coconut milk
1	cup plus 2 Tbsp. maple or date sugar
2	Tbsp. unsalted butter, melted
½	cup unsweetened shredded coconut
1/8	tsp. ground cinnamon

1. Preheat oven to 350°F. Butter a 9-in. pie dish.

2. Mix raisins and rum in a small bowl.

3. Whisk flour, nutmeg, and salt together in another small bowl.

4. In a large bowl, combine the mashed sweet potatoes and eggs and beat with an electric mixer on medium speed. Add coconut milk, 1 cup of the sugar, and the butter. Beat until combined.

5. Stir in flour mixture. Mix well.

6. Stir in raisins and rum.

7. Spread batter in dish.

8. Combine shredded coconut, remaining sugar, and cinnamon in a small bowl. Sprinkle on top of pie.

9. Bake until knife inserted in center comes out clean, about 1 hour. Let cool 15 minutes before serving.

Oat Chocolate Chip Cookies

I made these when I was experimenting with Dorie Greenspan's chocolate chip cookie recipe from Baking: From My Home to Yours. *I replaced the regular flour with oat flour and used maple sugar instead of regular sugar. To my surprise, they turned out very well and the kids loved them!*

Makes 20 cookies

1	cup unsalted butter, softened
1 2/3	cup maple sugar
2	large eggs
2	tsp. pure vanilla extract
2	cups oat flour
1	tsp. sea salt
¾	tsp. baking soda
12	oz. bittersweet chocolate chips or chunks

1. Preheat oven to 375°F. Line 2 or 3 baking sheets with silicone mats or parchment.

2. In a mixer, beat butter and sugar until soft and light. Add the eggs, one at a time, followed by the vanilla.

3. Meanwhile, sift flour, salt, and baking soda together into a bowl.

4. Reduce mixer speed to low and add the flour mixture in 3 intervals. When all the flour is added, increase the mixer speed to high for 1 minute.

5. Remove bowl from mixer and stir in chocolate chips or chunks (if using).

6. Using a tablespoon, spoon the dough onto the baking sheets about 2 in. apart.

7. Bake the cookies for 8-10 minutes, turning the baking sheet halfway through. If you are putting two baking sheets in the oven at once, rotate them halfway through.

8. Remove the cookies from the oven, allow to cool a little and, then transfer them to a wire rack to cool completely.

Real Carrot Cake

My mother used to make this cake when I was young. I love the combination of hazelnuts and carrots. I call this real carrot cake because it is simply carrots, nuts, and fruit. Super simple and super delicious.

Serves 6

4	large eggs
1	cup maple sugar
1	cup hazelnuts, ground
1	cup carrots, peeled and grated
½	cup raisins
1	tsp. lemon zest
1	Tbsp. fresh lemon juice
½	cup organic unbleached all-purpose flour
1	tsp. aluminum-free baking powder
1	Tbsp. confectioners' sugar for dusting (optional)

1. Preheat oven to 400°F. Butter a 9-in. springform pan.

2. Separate eggs.

3. In a large bowl, beat yolks and ½ cup of the sugar until creamy.

4. Combine hazelnuts, carrots, raisins, lemon zest, lemon juice, flour, and baking powder in a bowl. Stir into yolk and sugar mixture.

5. In a separate bowl, using clean beaters, beat egg whites with remaining sugar until stiff.

6. Fold egg whites into hazelnut and carrot mixture.

7. Bake for 50-60 minutes. Let cool and then sprinkle with confectioners' sugar (if using).

Apple Crisp

The best apples to use in this dish are the ones you pick yourself, like Macintosh, Cortland, or Braeburn, even though any type of apple will work in a pinch.

Serves 6

1	cup maple sugar
1	vanilla bean, split lengthwise
1	cup plus 1½ Tbsp. oat flour
1	Tbsp. fresh lemon juice
2	lb. apples, each peeled and cut into 8 wedges
1/8	tsp. ground cinnamon
	Pinch of sea salt
½	cup chilled, unsalted butter, cut into small cubes

1. Preheat the oven to 400°F and butter an 8x8-in. glass baking dish.

2. Place 1/3 cup of the sugar in a large bowl. Scrape seeds of vanilla bean into the bowl and combine well with sugar. Add 1½ Tbsp. of the oat flour and the lemon juice and mix well. Add the apples and stir to coat.

3. Put apple mixture into the baking dish and bake until apples are soft, about 20 minutes. Remove from oven and stir.

4. For the topping, mix the remaining 1 cup flour and 2/3 cup sugar, the cinnamon, and salt in a large bowl. Cut butter into flour mixture until it resembles coarse crumbs. Sprinkle over apples.

5. Return to oven and bake until crumbs are golden brown, another 20-25 minutes.

Sticky Date Cake

A close friend of mine gave me this recipe, which I tweaked slightly. Nothing beats the combination of dates and caramel.

Serves 6-8

1¼	cups pitted dates, chopped
1¼	cups boiling water
1	tsp. baking soda
¼	cup unsalted butter
¾	cup maple sugar
2	large eggs
1	cup whole-wheat pastry flour

For the caramel sauce

½	cup palm sugar
½	cup heavy cream
½	cup unsalted butter

1. Preheat oven to 350°F and butter a 9-in. round Bundt pan.

2. Put dates in a bowl and cover with the boiling water. Let stand for 5 minutes and add baking soda. Blend in a food processor until smooth.

3. In the food processor or in a large bowl with a hand mixer, cream butter and sugar until soft and light. Beat in eggs one at a time.

4. Add flour and date mixture and mix well.

5. Pour into the pan and bake for 45-60 minutes, or until a toothpick inserted in the center comes out clean.

6. Combine all the ingredients for the caramel sauce in a small saucepan. Stir until warm and sugar is dissolved.

7. Simmer 3 minutes. Let cool.

8. Let cake cool before inverting onto a plate.

9. Drizzle caramel sauce over cake.

Strawberry-Rhubarb Crumble

This is yet another take on a crisp or crumb cake and is interesting because rhubarb and strawberries are such a nice combination of sweet and tart.

Serves 6

¾ cup oat flour

⅔ cup, plus ½ cup maple sugar

½ cup rolled oats

½ cup blanched, slivered unsalted almonds

Pinch of sea salt

6 Tbsp. unsalted butter, cut into small cubes

½ vanilla bean, split lengthwise and seeds scraped

1 lb. strawberries, hulled and halved

1 lb. rhubarb, cut into ½-in. pieces

1. Preheat oven to 375°F and butter a 9x5-in. baking dish.

2. Combine flour, ⅔ cup sugar, oats, almonds, and salt in a bowl. Mix well. Cut butter into flour mixture until it resembles coarse crumbs.

3. In a large bowl, mix ½ cup sugar with vanilla seeds. Add strawberries and rhubarb. Mix well.

4. Scrape fruit into pan and sprinkle oat topping over fruit.

5. Bake 45 minutes, until filling bubbles. Let cool 15 minutes, then serve.

Cranberry Upside-Down Cake

I like this cake because the cranberries give it a hint of tartness. If you prefer, you can use other fruit, such as pineapple, pears, or plums. If you are using pineapples, you can arrange ½-in. slices in circles around the bottom of the pan, and if you are using pears or plums, you can cut them in wedges and arrange them around the bottom of the pan.

Serves 6

1¾	cups maple sugar
2	Tbsp. unsalted butter
2	Tbsp. plus ¼ cup fresh orange juice
3	cups cranberries (or other fruit)
¾	cup whole-wheat pastry flour
¾	cup unbleached all-purpose flour
2	tsp. aluminum-free baking powder
¼	tsp. sea salt
2	large eggs
⅓	cup plus 2 Tbsp. unsalted butter, melted
1	tsp. pure vanilla extract
½	cup organic, unhomogenized whole milk

1. Preheat oven to 350°F.

2. Heat ¾ cup of the sugar, butter and 2 Tbsp. orange juice in a small pan to make a caramel mixture. Bring to a boil and pour around edge of a 9-in. round cake pan.

3. Bring the remaining ¼ cup orange juice and cranberries to a simmer and cook until the half the cranberries have popped, 6-7 minutes. Pour on top of caramel mixture in cake pan.

4. Whisk flours, baking powder, and salt in a large bowl.

5. Separate eggs.

6. Place yolks, melted butter, the remaining 1 cup sugar, and vanilla in the bowl of a stand mixer. Mix until light and fluffy, about 8 minutes.

7. Stir in half of flour mixture then half of milk. Repeat.

8. In a medium bowl with clean beaters, beat the egg whites until they hold stiff

CONTINUED >

peaks. Fold into batter and spread batter over cranberries.

9. Bake 30-40 minutes, until knife inserted in center comes out clean and cake pulls away from the sides of the pan.

10. Cool to room temperature. Gently run a knife around the edge of the pan, cover the pan with a plate, and invert. Turn the cake right side up by inverting onto another plate.

Mango Yogurt Mousse

This dessert might seem heavy because of the yogurt and cream, but it actually is very light and refreshing. If you can find it, unsweetened mango purée works well for this recipe. If not, I suggest using very ripe mangoes.

Serves 6

1	Tbsp. agar flakes
2	cups mango purée (from 2 very ripe peeled and pitted mangoes)
1/3	cup maple sugar
1/2	tsp. pure vanilla extract
1	cup plain full-fat yogurt
1	cup heavy cream
	Mango slices and raspberries

1. Sprinkle agar flakes over 1/4 cup cold water, let soften 1 minute. Heat mixture on stovetop to dissolve flakes and thicken.

2. In a blender, combine mango purée, sugar, vanilla, and agar flakes. Transfer to bowl and stir in yogurt.

3. In a medium bowl, beat cream until it holds stiff peaks. Fold into mango mixture. Pour into individual serving bowls or a large bowl (I prefer to use martini glasses). Chill overnight.

4. Garnish with raspberries and mint and serve.

Cherry and Almond Clafouti

Like the Far Breton (see recipe on p. 264), a clafouti is essentially a sweetened custard with fruit. The most traditional fruit is cherries but you can use other fruit, such as blackberries or pears. Adding almonds gives a nice texture to the dish.

Serves 6-8

3	cups fruit (pitted cherries, blackberries, or peeled and cubed pears)
¾	cup almond milk (or organic, unhomogenized whole milk)
½	cup unsalted butter, melted
3	large eggs, beaten lightly
1	tsp. pure vanilla extract
½	tsp. pure almond extract
½	cup almond flour
¾	cup oat flour
½	cup plus 2 Tbsp. maple sugar
	Pinch of sea salt
¼	cup slivered almonds

1. Preheat the oven to 400°F.

2. Butter a 9-in. round glass pie dish and place fruit in dish.

3. Combine almond milk, butter, eggs, and vanilla and almond extracts in a blender and mix well.

4. Combine almond flour, oat flour, ½ cup sugar, and salt in a medium bowl. Add to milk and egg mixture and blend well.

5. Pour batter over fruit. Sprinkle slivered almonds and remaining sugar over cake.

6. Bake for 40 minutes, or until puffed and browned, and a knife inserted in the center comes out clean.

7. Let cool and serve.

 If using pears, rub them with fresh lemon juice so they do not turn brown while you are preparing the rest of the ingredients.

Far Breton

This is one of my favorite French cakes because I like its custardy texture.
I like to serve it for brunch. It is very similar to Cherry and Almond Clafouti
(see recipe on p. 263), and you can use cherries or blackberries in the place of
the dried fruit (and omit the tea) if you wanted to make a clafouti instead.

Serves 6

1	cup pitted prunes
⅓	cup raisins
1	cup Earl Grey tea, hot
3	large eggs
2	cups organic unhomogenized whole milk
½	cup maple sugar
¼	tsp. pure vanilla extract
⅛	tsp. sea salt
5	Tbsp. unsalted butter, melted and cooled to room temperature; more for pan
¾	cup barley flour or unbleached organic all-purpose flour

1. Put the prunes and raisins in a bowl and cover with the hot tea. Allow to cool to room temperature.

2. Put the eggs, milk, sugar, vanilla, salt, and melted butter in a bowl and stir to mix ingredients.

3. Add the flour and whisk until well blended. Refrigerate batter overnight.

4. Preheat the oven to 375°F. Butter a 9x2-in. round cake pan and line the bottom with parchment.

5. Remove the batter from the refrigerator. Whisk to blend and pour into cake pan. Drain the fruit and scatter evenly over the batter.

6. Bake 50-60 minutes, until the top of the cake is puffed and browned, and a knife inserted in the center comes out clean.

7. Cool to room temperature. Gently run a knife around the edge of the pan, cover the pan with a plate and invert. Turn the cake right side up by inverting onto another plate. If you'd like, for single-serving portions, cut out rounds using a circular cookie cutter.

Coconut Rice Pudding

While I like regular rice pudding, especially in winter, this version is good because the coconut milk gives it additional flavor and creaminess. On occasion, I like to add dried fruit, such as raisins, to give it more texture.

Serves 6

¾	cup Arborio (or any short-grain) rice
6	cups almond milk
3	cups coconut milk
¼	cup palm sugar
1	Tbsp. pure vanilla extract
1	tsp. sea salt
3	Tbsp. cinnamon sugar (3 Tbsp. maple sugar and 1 tsp. ground cinnamon)
½	cup shredded coconut, toasted (optional)
1	mango, diced, for garnish

1. Put rice in a pot and rinse under cold water. Drain the rice and soak it in cold water for 1 hour. Drain again.

2. Put the rice, milks, sugar, vanilla, and salt in a medium saucepan. Heat until boiling. Reduce heat to low, partially cover pan and simmer for 1 hour, stirring occasionally.

3. Sprinkle with cinnamon sugar, shredded coconut (if using), and diced mango.

Blueberry Crumb Cake

I love this recipe because the fruit softens and melts into the cake and makes it so delicious. You can also make this dish with pitted cherries or blackberries.

Serves 6

½	lb. unsalted butter, softened
1½	cups maple sugar
2	tsp. pure vanilla extract
3	large eggs plus 3 large yolks
¼	cup buttermilk or organic unhomogenized whole milk
2½	cups organic unbleached all-purpose flour
2	tsp. aluminum-free baking powder
4	cups blueberries

For the crumb topping

2	cups organic unbleached all-purpose flour
²/₃	cup maple sugar
½	tsp. ground cinnamon
¼	tsp. ground nutmeg
¾	cup unsalted butter, melted

1. Preheat oven to 350°F. Butter a 9x5-in. glass or ceramic baking dish.

2. In a large bowl, beat butter, and sugar, vanilla until soft and light. Add the whole eggs one at a time, beating well after each addition.

3. Stir yolks into buttermilk or milk.

4. Sift together flour and baking powder and stir into butter mixture in three additions, alternating with yolk and milk mixture. Spread batter in baking dish.

5. Scatter blueberries over batter and lightly press them in.

6. To make crumb topping, mix flour, sugar, cinnamon, and nutmeg in bowl. Stir in melted butter and use fingertips to form coarse crumbs. Scatter crumbs over berries as evenly as possible.

7. Bake cake 45-60 minutes, or until a toothpick inserted in the center comes out clean.

Resources

RESOURCES

BIBLIOGRAPHY

Allport, Susan. (2006). *The Queen of Fats: Why omega-3s were removed from the western diet and what we can do to replace them.* Berkeley: University of California Press.

Blaylock, Russell, M.D. (1997). *Excitotoxins: The Taste That Kills.* Santa Fe, New Mexico: Health Press

Bittman, Mark. (2009). *Food Matters: A guide to conscious eating with more than 75 recipes.* New York: Simon & Schuster.

Bowden, Jonny, Ph.D., C.N.S. (2008). *The Most Effective Natural Cures on Earth.* Gloucester, Massachusetts: Fair Winds Press.

Bowden, Jonny, Ph.D., C.N.S. (2007). *The 150 Healthiest Foods on Earth.* Gloucester, Massachusetts: Fair Winds Press.

Campbell, T. Colin and Campbell, Thomas M. II. (2006). *The China Study: The most comprehensive study of nutrition ever conducted and the startling implications for diet, weight loss and long-term health.* Dallas, Texas: BenBella Books.

Centers for Disease Control and Prevention (October, 2008). *Food Allergy Among U.S. Children: trends in prevalence and hospitalizations.* NCHS Data Brief, 10.

Centers for Disease Control and Prevention (February, 2012). *Fourth National Report on Human Exposure to Environmental Chemicals.* Retrieved from Centers for Disease Control and Prevention website: www.cdc.gov/exposurereport

Centers for Disease Control and Prevention, NCHS Data Brief (January 2012). *U.S. obesity trends.* Retrieved from website: www.cdc.gov/obesity/data/trends.html

Chivian, Eric and Bernstein, Aaron, eds. (2008). *Sustaining Life: how human health depends on biodiversity.* Oxford: Oxford University Press.

Colbin, Annemarie. (1986). *Food and Healing: how what you eat determines your health, your well-being, and the quality of your life.* New York: Ballantine Books.

Colbin, Annemarie. (September, 1997). *Fat-free Food: A bad idea.* Retrieved from website: www.foodandhealing.com/articles/article-fatfreebad.htm

Colbin, Annemarie. (2009). *The Whole-Food Guide to Strong Bones: A holistic approach.* Oakland, California: New Harbinger Publications.

Daniel, Kaayla T., Ph.D., C.C.N. (2005). *The Whole Soy Story: The dark side of America's favorite health food.* Washington, DC: NewTrends Publishing.

Dufty, William. (1986). *Sugar Blues.* New York: Grand Central Publishing.

Environmental Working Group. (2012). *EWG's Shopper's Guide to Pesticides.* http://www.ewg.org/foodnews/

Fallon, Sally with Enig, Mary G., Ph.D. (2001). *Nourishing traditions: The cookbook that challenges politically correct nutrition and the diet dictocrats.* Washington, DC: NewTrends Publishing.

Grescoe, Taras. (2008). *Bottomfeeder: How to eat ethically in a world of vanishing seafood.* New York: Bloomsbury USA.

Haas, Elson M., M.D. with Levin, Buck, Ph.D., R.D. (2006). *Staying healthy with nutrition, revised: the complete guide to diet and nutritional medicine.* Berkeley: Celestial Arts.

Hoffmann, David, F.N.I.M.H., A.H.G. (2003). *Medical herbalism: the science and practice of herbal medicine.* Rochester, Vermont: Healing Arts Press.

Isaacson, Walter. *Steve Jobs.* (New York: Little, Brown, 2011) p. 31, 36.

Keay, John. (2006). *The spice route: a history.* Berkeley: University of California Press.

Kimbrell, Andrew. (2007). *Your right to know: genetic engineering and the secret changes in your food.* San Rafael, CA: Earth Aware Editions.

Kurlansky, Mark. (2002). *Salt: A world history.* New York: Walker and Co..

Nestle, Marion. (2006). *What to Eat.* New York: North Point Press.

O'Brien, Robyn with Kranz, Rachel. (2009). *The Unhealthy Truth: How our food is making us sick and what we can do about it.* New York: Broadway Books.

Planck, Nina. (2006). *Real Food: What to eat and why.* New York: Bloomsbury USA.

Pollan, Michael. (2009). *Food Rules: An eater's manual.* New York: Penguin Books.

Pollan, Michael. (2008). *In Defense of food: an eater's manifesto.* New York: Penguin Books.

Pollan, Michael. (2006). *The Omnivore's Dilemma: A natural history of four meals.* New York: Penguin Books.

Price, Weston A., D.D.S. (2008). *Nutrition and Physical Degeneration, 8th Edition.* La Mesa, CA: Price-Pottenger Nutrition Foundation.

Rimas, Andrew and Fraser, Evan D.G. (2008). *Beef: the untold story of how milk, meat, and muscle shaped the world.* New York: William Morrow.

Smith, Jeffrey M. (2003). *Seeds of Deception: Exposing industry and government lies about the safety of the genetically engineered foods you're eating.* Fairfield, IA: Yes! Books.

Tillotson, Alan Keith, Ph.D., A.H.G., D.Ay., with Tillotson, Nai-shing Hu, O.M.D., L.Ac., and Abel, Robert Jr., M.D. (2001). *The One Earth Herbal Sourcebook: Everything you need to know about Chinese, Western, and Ayurvedic herbal treatments.* New York: Kensington Publishing Group.

Tompkins, Peter and Bird, Christopher. (1973). *The Secret Life of Plants.* New York: Harper & Row.

Wrangham, Richard. (2009). *Catching Fire: How cooking made us human.* New York: Basic Books.

RESOURCES

ENDNOTES

PART ONE

p. 12
1) Centers for Disease Control and Prevention. *U.S. Obesity Trends.* www.cdc.gov/obesity/data/trends.html.

p. 13
2) Centers for Disease Control and Prevention. (2008). *Food Allergy Among U.S. Children: Trends in Prevalence and Hospitalizations*, NCHS Data Brief, October 2008, No. 10. www.cdc.gov.

p. 21
3) Lad, Vasant, B.A.M.S., M.A.Sc., *The Complete Book of Ayurvedic Home Remedies.* (New York: Three Rivers Press, 1998) pp.15-29.

p. 22
4) Isaacson Walter, *Steve Jobs* (London: Little, Brown, 2011) p. 31, 36.

p. 32
5) Dufty, William, *Sugar Blues* (New York: Grand Central Publishing, 1975) p.137.

p. 32
6) Colbin, Annemarie. *Food and Healing* (New York: Ballantine Books, 1986) p.156.

p. 32
7) Nestle, Marion. *What to Eat* (New York: North Point Press, 2006) p.81.

p. 33
8) Blaylock, Russell, M.D. *Excitotoxins: The Taste That Kills.* (Santa Fe, New Mexico: Health Press, 1997) p. 31.

PART TWO

p. 43
9) Bernstein, Aaron and Chivian, Eric, eds. *Sustaining Life: How Human Health Depends on Biodiversity* (Oxford: Oxford University Press, 2008) p.59.

p. 43
10) Nestle, Marion, p.465.

p. 43
11) Bernstein and Chivian, p.397.

p. 43
12) United States Department of Agriculture, National Agricultural Library. http://www.nal.usda.gov/afsic/pubs/ofp/ofp.shtml.

p. 43
13) Organic Trade Association, "*Organic Agriculture and Production.*" www.ota.com.

p. 46
14) Bernstein and Chivian, p.330.

p. 48
15) Nestle, pp.176-177.

p. 49
16) United Nations Food and Agriculture Organization, *Depleted fish stocks require recovery efforts*, 7 March 2005. http://www.fao.org/newsroom/en/news/2005/100095/index.html.

p. 50
17) Grescoe, Taras. *Bottomfeeders: How to Eat Ethically in a World of Vanishing Seafood.* (New York: Bloomsbury Press, 2008) p.2.

p. 50
18) Ibid., p.25.

p. 51
19) Ibid., pp. 242-246.

p. 52
20) Annemarie Colbin, "*Fat Free Food: A Bad Idea*" Free Spirit Magazine, Sept. 1997.

p. 54
21) Enig, Mary G., PhD. *Know Your Fats: The Complete Primer for Understanding the Nutrition of Fats, Oils and Cholesterol.* (Maryland: Bethesda Press, 2000) pp.99-100.

p. 54
22) Nestle, p.112.

p. 55
23) Fallon, Sally and Enig, Mary G., PhD. *Nourishing Traditions: The Cookbook that Challenges Politically Correct Nutrition and the Diet Dictocrats.* (Washington, DC: New Trends Publishing, 2001) pp.34-35.

p. 55
24) O'Brien, Robyn, with Kranz, Rachel. *The Unhealthy Truth: How Our Food is Making Us Sick – and What We Can Do About It.* (New York: Broadway Books, 2009) p. 98.

p. 60
25) Nestle, p.310.

p. 60
26) Pollan, Michael. *In Defense of Food: An Eater's Manifesto.* (New York: The Penguin Press, 2008) p.117.

p. 60
27) *USDA National Agricultural Statistical Service 2009 Crop Year is One for the Record Books*, 12 January 2010.

http://www.nass.usda.gov/Newsroom/2010/-01_12_2010.asp.

p. 61
28) Fallon and Enig, p.62.

p. 63
29) Smith, Jeffrey M. *Seeds of Deception: Exposing Industry and Government Lies About the Safety of the Genetically Modified Foods You're Eating.* (Fairfield, CT: Yes! Books, 2003) pp. 47-70.

p. 63
30) Ibid, p.59.

PART THREE

p. 66
31) Price, Weston A., DDS. *Nutrition and Physical Degeneration*, 8th Edition. (California: The Price-Pottenger Nutrition Foundation, 2008) p.1.

p. 67
32) Pollan, Michael Pollan, Michael. *Food Rules: An Eater's Manual.* (New York: The Penguin Group, 2009) p. xvii.

p. 69
33) Haas, Elson M., MD with Levin, Buck, PhD, RD. *Staying Healthy with Nutrition: The Complete Guide to Diet and Nutritional Medicine.* (Berkeley, Toronto: Celestial Press, 2006) p.146.

p. 117
34) Hanna Kroeger. *Ageless Remedies from Mother's Kitchen*, 4th Edition. (Boulder, Colorado: Hanna Kroeger Publications, 1981). p.19.

p. 117
35) Bowden, Jonny, PhD, CNS. *The Most Effective Natural Cures on Earth.* (Gloucester, Massachusetts: Fairwinds Press, 2008) pp.189-190.

ADDITIONAL RESOURCES

Documentaries

- **Fast Food Nation**, 2006, directed by Richard Linklater

- **Food Inc.**, 2008, directed by Robert Kenner

- **Fresh: The Movie**, 2009, directed by Ana Sofia Joanes

- **King Corn**, 2007, directed by Aaron Wolf

- **The Cove**, 2009, directed by Louie Psihoyos

- **The Future of Food**, 2004, directed by Deborah Koons Garcia

- **Two Angry Moms**, 2007, directed by Amy Kalafa and Alex Gunuey

Websites

- www.healthytiffin.net
- www.ewg.org/food-news
- www.angrymoms.org
- www.montereybay-aquarium.org/cr/sea-foodwatch.aspx
- www.hsph.harvard.edu/nutritionsource/
- www.drweil.com

RECIPE INDEX

INDEX

NOTE: Page numbers in *italics* indicate photographs.

continued

continued

continued

NOTES

NOTES